TED
HUGHES

THOMAS WEST

METHUEN
LONDON AND NEW YORK

*This book is dedicated to my mother
and to the memory of my father
TGW*

*First published in 1985 by
Methuen & Co. Ltd
11 New Fetter Lane, London EC4P 4EE
Published in the USA by
Methuen & Co.
in association with Methuen, Inc.
29 West 35th Street, New York, NY 10001*

© *1985 Thomas West*

*Typeset by Rowland Phototypesetting Ltd
Printed in Great Britain by
Richard Clay (The Chaucer Press) Ltd
Bungay, Suffolk*

British Library Cataloguing in Publication Data

*West, Thomas
Ted Hughes. – (Contemporary writers)
1. Hughes, Ted – Criticism and interpretation
I. Title   II. Series
821'.914   PR6058.U37Z/*

ISBN 0-416-35400-9

Library of Congress Cataloging in Publication Data

*West, Thomas, 1948–
Ted Hughes.
(Contemporary writers)
Bibliography: p.
1. Hughes, Ted, 1930–   – Criticism and interpretation.
I. Title   II. Series.
PR6058.U37Z94   1985   821'.914   85-11592*

ISBN 0-416-35400-9 (pbk.)

CHRISTOPHER BIGSBY

TED HUGHES

CONTENTS

GENERAL EDITORS' PREFACE

The contemporary is a country which we all inhabit, but there is little agreement as to its boundaries or its shape. The serious writer is one of its most sensitive interpreters, but criticism is notoriously cautious in offering a response or making a judgement. Accordingly, this continuing series is an endeavour to look at some of the most important writers of our time, and the questions raised by their work. It is, in effect, an attempt to map the contemporary, to describe its aesthetic and moral topography.

The series came into existence out of two convictions. One was that, despite all the modern pressures on the writer and on literary culture, we live in a major creative time, as vigorous and alive in its distinctive way as any that went before. The other was that, though criticism itself tends to grow more theoretical and apparently indifferent to contemporary creation, there are grounds for a lively aesthetic debate. This series, which includes books written from various standpoints, is meant to provide a forum for that debate. By design, some of those who have contributed are themselves writers, willing to respond to their contemporaries; others are critics who have brought to the discussion of current writing the spirit of contemporary criticism or simply a conviction, forcibly and coherently argued, for the contemporary significance of their subjects. Our aim, as the series develops, is to continue to explore the works of major post-war writers – in fiction, drama and poetry – over an international range, and thereby to illuminate not only those works but also in some degree the artistic, social and moral assumptions on which they rest. Our wish is that, in their very variety of approach and emphasis, these books will stimulate interest in and understanding of the vitality of a living literature which, because it is contemporary, is especially ours.

Norwich, England   MALCOLM BRADBURY
                                                      CHRISTOPHER BIGSBY

PREFACE AND ACKNOWLEDGEMENTS

I doubt whether anyone would challenge the assertion that Ted Hughes has been one of our most important poets since the appearance of *Crow* in 1970. His work has long been studied in universities, polytechnics and secondary schools. That some readers dislike Ted Hughes's poetry, distrusting his vatic view of the art or believing more in a writer's obligations to his immediate surroundings, is also a matter of fact. They suspect his gratuitous violence and his apparent refusal of complicity with the world as it exists. For many of those who admire him, the same qualities are viewed in an opposite light, so that Hughes becomes a 'nature poet' or an 'animal poet' who has turned towards an untamed, unsocial world for inspiration and guidance. Both reactions perhaps show how Hughes's work has drawn up the old battle-lines of poetic engagement between those who trust fictions of the everyday world and those who have been visited by truths un-available to ordinary, jaded senses – the same lines, more or less, with which our century began, Georgians on one side, Modernists on the other. The familiar debate is not easy to put aside, for it concerns, ultimately, a timeless debate about values and the value of fictions.

In the event, I have felt in writing this book that the best way is to avoid these camps and convictions as much as possible and explore what I believe to be the main impulse of Hughes's poetry. My principal concern has been to clarify the poet's own subjective relationship to his writing and the problems this presents to the reader. Trying to understand this subjective point of view has taken my argument into Hughes's biographical and intellectual origins, and to questions more primitive than poetry itself but central to understanding his vision – questions like 'What is a mythic utterance?', 'What purpose does myth serve?' and 'Where does the myth-maker get his knowledge from?'

The dramatic relationship between two narrative voices, which is typical of Hughes's work, rests on precisely such questions. One voice expresses the ordinary man, at once unknowing and intimidated, yet conscious of larger forces; the other expresses a superior or preternatural vision. Behind these two narrative voices is the moving force of the poet himself, who, through the tragedy of his advocates' drama, is always seeking to forge a new, single self, a re-organ-ization which will bridge the eons of time that, according to Hughes, separate the natural animal and the human animal. I have followed the evolution of this tragic drama more or less chronologically, from the early work to the radical poetry and theatre of the late 1960s and early 1970s, and then to the increasingly sensuous writing of recent works such as *Gaudete*, *Moortown*, *Remains of Elmet*, *River* and *What is the Truth?*

It is a special pleasure for me to thank here my friend Victor Sage who has helped along and imparted velocity to many a lumbering thought. My thanks go as well to my colleagues Malcolm Bradbury and Christopher Bigsby for their help and advice throughout.

*

The author and the publisher would like to thank the following for permission to reproduce copyright material: Faber & Faber Ltd and Harper & Row, Inc. for extracts from Ted Hughes's *The Hawk in the Rain*, *Lupercal*, *Wodwo*, *Crow*, *Gaudete*, *Remains of Elmet*, *Moortown*, *River* and *What is the Truth?* Faber & Faber Ltd and Doubleday, Inc. for extracts from *Seneca's 'Oedipus'* and *Poetry in the Making* by Ted Hughes and *A Choice of Shakespeare's Verse* edited by Ted Hughes; Faber & Faber Ltd and Viking Press, Inc. for extracts from *Cave Birds* by Ted Hughes. Faber & Faber Ltd and Farrar, Straus & Giroux for an extract from *High Windows* by Philip Larkin; Robert Graves for two extracts from *The White Goddess*.

A NOTE ON THE TEXTS

Page references for quotations are taken from the British editions listed in the Bibliography, unless otherwise stated. The following abbreviations have been used:

Works by Ted Hughes:

HR	*The Hawk in the Rain*
L	*Lupercal*
W	*Wodwo*
O	*Seneca's 'Oedipus'*
C	*Crow*
G	*Gaudete*
CB	*Cave Birds*
RE	*Remains of Elmet*
M	*Moortown*
R	*River*
WT	*What is the Truth?*

PM	*Poetry in the Making*
Shakespeare	*A Choice of Shakespeare's Verse*
Myth I	'Myth and Education' (1970)
Myth II	'Myth and Education' (1976)
Interview I	'Ted Hughes and *Crow*'
Interview II	'Ted Hughes and *Gaudete*'
NT	*Ted Hughes and R. S. Thomas Read and Discuss Selections of Their Own Poems* (Norwich Tapes)

Other publications:

Art	Keith Sagar, *The Art of Ted Hughes*
Achievement	Keith Sagar (ed.), *The Achievement of Ted Hughes*
Creative Mythology	Joseph Campbell, *Creative Mythology* (Harmondsworth: Penguin, 1976)
Dictionary	Charles Winick, *Dictionary of Anthropology* (Totowa, NJ: Littlefield, Adams, 1970)
Orghast	A. C. H. Smith, *Orghast at Persepolis* (London: Eyre Methuen, 1972)
Thomas Hardy and British Poetry	Donald Davie, *Thomas Hardy and British Poetry* (London: Routledge & Kegan Paul, 1973)
Study	T. Gifford and N. Roberts, *Ted Hughes: A Critical Study*
WG	Robert Graves, *The White Goddess* (London: Faber, 1961)

1

ORIGINS

Civilization is comparatively new, it is still a bit of a strain on our nerves ... the meaning of our experience is finally unfathomable, it reaches into our toes and back to before we were born and into the atom ... words tend to shut out the simplest things we wish to say. In a way, words are continually trying to displace our experience ... and full of themselves and all the dictionaries they have digested, they do displace it. ... The struggle truly to possess his own experience, in other words to regain his genuine self, has been man's principal occupation, wherever he could find leisure for it, ever since he first grew this enormous surplus of brain. (*PM*, pp. 76, 119, 120, 124)

Edward James Hughes was born on 17 August 1930 in Mytholmroyd, on one of England's first industrialized rivers, the Calder, in the Yorkshire Pennines. By tradition his mother, Edith Farrar, traced ancestry back to Foxe's famous martyr, Bishop Farrar (treated in one of Hughes's early poems). His father, William Hughes, was a carpenter, one of only seventeen out of a whole regiment to have escaped death at Gallipoli in the First World War (also treated in several early poems – 'Bayonet Charge', 'Griefs for Dead Soldiers' and 'Six Young Men', *HR*, pp. 51–5). The rundown Calder Valley seems to have left a far greater impression than Mexborough, where the family moved when Ted was only seven years old. For him the Calder Valley represents the first part of rural England to be tamed by John Wesley (in 1736). It is remembered as a sinister staging-post between the great mill towns of Lancashire and Yorkshire. But, perhaps most important for the poet, the valley also contains remnants of the 'last British Celtic Kingdom to fall to the Angles' (*RE*, p. 8), that is, a kind of extinct, mythic homeland.

In South Yorkshire, where the father ran a newsagent's and tobacconist's shop, the schoolboy showed a flair for English and was writing poetry from the age of 15. Before leaving on an Open

Exhibition to Cambridge, Hughes was given, as a prize from his grammar school, Robert Graves's *The White Goddess*, which had first appeared in 1946. This undoubtedly represents the most, if not the only, influential work by another writer to impress itself deeply on his whole poetic career.

Choosing to do National Service first, Hughes finally arrived at Cambridge in 1951 and, after disappointment with English, switched to follow an honours course in archaeology and anthropology. After graduating he went to work in London, drifting through a number of jobs, including zoo attendant (cf. 'The Jaguar' and 'Macaw and Little Miss', *HR*, pp. 12–13) and reader for J. Arthur Rank. Before publishing his first book, *The Hawk in the Rain*, he met in Cambridge the American poet Sylvia Plath, who had come on a Fulbright Scholarship to read English. The two were married later that year (1956) and went to the USA in 1957, where Sylvia taught literature at Smith College and Ted taught English and Creative Writing at the University of Massachussetts in Amherst. The couple toured the country in 1959, then spent several months in the writers' colony of Yaddo in Saratoga Springs, NY before returning to England in December 1959.

They settled in London until August, both leading productive literary lives, Sylvia publishing *The Colossus*, Ted, *Lupercal*. Their first child, Frieda Rebecca, was born in April 1960. Gradually Ted grew tired of the city, and in September 1961 the family moved to Devon where they had bought an old rectory (where the poet still lives). A second child came in 1962, Nicholas Farrar, yet by the middle of the year the marriage was in trouble. Hughes had an affair with another person and, shortly afterwards, Sylvia attempted to commit suicide. The two moved, separately, back to London where Sylvia died by gas asphyxiation in February 1963.

Little has been told about Hughes in the wake of this event. The eloquence of his laments, 'The Howling of Wolves', 'Song of a Rat' and a fragmentary play from which 'Ghost Crabs', and the third part of 'Gog' derive (written in 1963, all published in *Wodwo* in 1967), suffices in the way of personal testimony. For nearly three years he stopped writing poetry altogether, publishing reviews and articles to stay afloat. After a trip to Ireland in 1966 he seemed to have recovered his force. But tragedy again descended in March 1969, when his companion Assia Gutsmann and their daughter Shura died. In 1970 Hughes married Carol Orchard, daughter of a mid-Devon farmer Hughes subsequently worked with in the 1970s, and whom he celebrated in the 'Moortown Elegies' of 1978. Around 1970 Hughes and several other writers got together to form The Arvon Foundation, to help promote young poets, novelists and dramatists. In the summer of 1971, following up previous collaboration with the director of the National Theatre, Peter Brook, Hughes went to Iran with Brook's new international company, to write a play for the theatrical section of that country's bimillenial celebrations. An avid fisherman, Hughes went to Alaska with his son Nicholas for the giant salmon in the summer of 1980. Only now, in a recent volume, *River*, are we beginning to develop a full idea of this side of the man, the angler and the naturalist. In December 1984 Hughes was named to succeed Sir John Betjeman as Poet Laureate.

On the surface, then, perhaps in contrast with so many poets whose very rooms encompass their major physical voyages, Hughes's life appears eventful and even turbulent. But to read this turbulence into his works would be only half pertinent. Of course, the dark tones of *Wodwo* (1967) and the urge that gave rise to *Crow* (1970) have to do with autobiography. But, the closer one looks, the more one is struck by the near absence of direct literary influence or biographical influence. In this respect Hughes is quite different from Sylvia Plath and from poets like Robert Lowell who have aligned subjectivity with a 'confessional mode'. When poems are of an admitted diary quality, as in some *Moortown* (1979) poems, that objective world to which autobiography and influence are related appears in a telling way: one that reveals the subtle difference between subjectivity and autobiography.

However, if in one sense Hughes's poetry is anti-autobiographical, it is, in a subjective sense, supremely and obsessively biographical, almost always functioning for the poet as a charm or a counter-magic against some problem that besets what the reader feels to be the poet's own lesser self, an ordinary, waking self. This pattern of response can be traced back through Hughes's writings to his childhood and represents a recurrent touchstone in his work. The familiar exteriors of ordinary autobiography, the sensuous world of 'facts', is assimilated, from the very beginning, into a world of struggle between opposing forces.

The first 'facts' – the poetic 'first principles' – which set in motion a creative response in the young Hughes seem to be associated both symbolically and literally with a sheer cliff in the Calder Valley, west of Halifax:

> I have heard that valley is notable for its suicides, which I can believe, and I could also believe that rock is partly to blame for them. . . . A slightly disastrous, crumbly, grey light, sunless and yet too clear, like a still from the documentary film of an accident. . . . All because of that rock and its evil eye.
>
> It had an evil eye, I have no doubt. For one thing you cannot look at a precipice without thinking instantly what it would be like to fall down it, or jump down it. Mountaineers are simply men who need to counter-attack on that thought. . . . Every thought I tried to send beyond the confines of the valley had to step over that high, definite hurdle. (*The Listener*, 19 September 1963)

What is striking about this passage is not just the attribution of a brooding eye with special powers to the landscape, but the way in which the sinister, charmed summit is felt to *demand* a human response. The result of this challenge, as Hughes's account makes clear, is a radical division of the reactions which are available to the imprisoned and oppressed human subject: on the one hand 'suicide' and, on the other, conquest or a 'counter-attack on that thought'. At some stage in life the young Hughes felt vividly the conflicting roles of this mental drama. And though retrospection has no doubt shaped the account, the simple 'fact' of Scout Rock reveals a quite complex reaction, in the form of mental repression or censure, which one recognizes in a number of staring or intimidating things in the early writings. The same feeling and the same stark alternatives are perhaps more familiar as expressed in Edgar Allan Poe's extraordinary essay in psychology, 'The Imp of the Perverse'. Like Hughes, Poe is contemplating the brink of a precipice:

> We peer into the abyss – we grow sick and dizzy. Our impulse is to shrink from the danger. Unaccountably we remain. By slow degrees our sickness and dizziness and horror become merged in a cloud of unnamable feeling. By gradations, still more imperceptible, this cloud assumes shape, as did the vapor from

16

the bottle out of which arose the genius in the Arabian Nights. But out of this *our* cloud upon the precipice's edge, there grows into palpability, a shape, far more terrible than any genius or any demon of a tale, and yet it is but a thought, although a fearful one, and one which chills the very marrow of our bones with the fierceness of the delight of its horror. It is merely the idea of what would be our sensations during the sweeping precipitancy of a fall from such a height. And this fall – this rushing annihilation – for the very reason that it involves that one most ghastly and loathsome of all the most ghastly and loathsome images of death and suffering which have ever presented themselves to our imagination – for this very cause do we now the most vividly desire it. And because our reason violently deters us from the brink, *therefore* do we the most impetuously approach it.

Poe tells us that the whole 'experience' of looking into the precipice is actually a violent but *unreal* thought – about something that lies beyond experience and thus beyond our ability to know (save, that is, for those who have actually taken the leap and know what they fear): 'and yet it is but a thought, although a fearful one'. For Hughes, on the contrary, the alternatives when faced with a similar obstacle of a natural form are extinction or conquest. Hughes's attitude differs not only from Poe's, who is ever distrustful of thoughts about shadows, but also from what one might be tempted to see as some echo of Romantic tradition: Wordsworth's 'eye that hath kept watch o'er man's mortality', for example, or the famous boating incident in the *Prelude* (ll. 81 ff.) when the 'huge cliff' rears up in front of the boy in the stolen shepherd's boat, the very emblem of his guilt and the agent of nature's tutoring spirit:

> It was an act of stealth
> And troubled pleasure. Not without the voice
> Of mountain echoes did my boat move on . . .
>
> And as I rose upon the stroke my boat
> Went heaving through the water like a swan –
> When from behind that rocky steep, till then
> The bound of the horizon, a huge cliff,
> As if with voluntary power instinct,

Upreared its head. I struck, and struck again,
And, growing still in stature, the huge cliff
Rose up between me and the stars, and still,
With measured motion, like a living thing
Strode after me . . . (I, ll. 90–2, 105–14)

Hughes's cliff differs from Poe's abyss and from Wordsworth's rocky steep by the nature of the evil eye that is attributed to it. This eye is felt as an inquiring and accusatory presence. What is distinctive about it is the pressure of division which weighs upon the human psyche. This is clearly more complicated than just an opposition between man and nature. The natural world is hostile or *un*natural in terms of what the ordinary 'natural' human can understand. Its evil eye forces the witness to be either a slave or a rebel. In the account of Scout Rock, Hughes by implication assimilates the poet to the rebel, the mountaineer, who counter-attacks the charm of the precipice, sending his thoughts or body over against the oppressive and aggressive limits of the staring natural world. Here poetry, a kind of mountaineering *against* the evil eye of the precipice, is seen as a combative and liberating force.

One of Hughes's earliest and best known poems, 'The Hawk in the Rain', first called 'The Hawk in the Storm' and written around the end of 1956, is based on a drama like the one we see before Scout Rock. In the poem, however, this drama has been considerably interiorized – to a point where it is perhaps not obvious that two opposing voices are speaking to one another. Yet the poem is one sustained and uncomfortable encounter between a revealed force, made evident in the hawk's 'still eye', and a mere human eye, which recognizes and feels intimidated by the force that has been brought into a momentary focus. Note, as well, how the stillness of the eye in both the poem and the recollection of Scout Rock really relates to a quite complex feeling of fascination or mental captivity rather than to tranquillity or natural equilibrium.

The poem is apparently narrated by the man who sees with the mere human eye, a rain-drenched person who finds himself in the great gob of a man-handled field ('ploughland'). Here, the eye of the hawk, like Scout Rock, seems to make the narrator himself feel ambivalent. And thus the reader may be confused. The speaker says that the eye 'polestars' the sea-drowner's endurance, that is, it

18

fixes at once the direction of his will, while establishing a polarity, an opposite pole to the flux below. The speaker is at once attracted and repelled (because threatened) by the eye, and imagines himself as the terrified and mesmerized victim of the hawk:

> and I,

> Bloodily grabbed dazed last-moment-counting
> Morsel in the earth's mouth, strain towards the master-
> Fulcrum of violence where the hawk hangs still.

But the reader senses that this 'I' belongs to a dramatic fiction and is only indirectly identified with the poet's person. This 'I' acts out momentarily the victim's role and commits a kind of suicide within the imagination. In any event the final lines of the poem present a quite different perspective on the hawk. The voice that speaks here is distant, almost like that of an omniscient narrator, stepping back from both the bloodily dazed 'I' and the intimidating hawk, which

> maybe in his own time meets the weather

> Coming the wrong way, suffers the air, hurled upside down

until the bird is imagined being destroyed by the storm's force as its extraordinary still eye crashes into the fields below.

The latter voice seems implicitly to know all about the eye which, just above, had 'grabbed' and 'dazed' the person of some other 'I'. This omniscient voice seems to predict the future destruction of the hawk, and thus to align itself with the superior powers which became momentarily apparent to the 'grabbed' and 'dazed' 'I'. In terms of Scout Rock, what is happening here is a poetic equivalent of sending one's thoughts into the precipice beneath the rock, against the evil eye. One can interpret this reaction as an attempt to reverse and usurp the threatening stare of the natural world by imaginative means. As such, the dramatic encounter of the dazed 'I' and the hawk's 'still eye' includes a switch of voices. One senses this not only in the changing tone of the poem but also in the extreme ambiguity of the syntax and punctuation.

For instance the full stop after 'hangs still' serves no grammatical purpose (it comes at the end of a phrase not a sentence), but rather makes a pause before we enter the prophetic relative clause in the subjunctive mood, 'That maybe in his own time. . . .' This shift in mood and apparently in speaker reveals clearly, I think, the dramatic function of the drowning victim's voice, which is replaced by a much more prescient, much more authoritative voice, knowledgeable about the ways of the wind and of the hawk.

'The Hawk in the Rain' is thus a transaction between perspectives and voices which are in tension. Sensual nature in this poem serves mainly as a set of counters for an inner drama which is the poet's real concern. In some storms, that is, rain may 'hack' one's 'head to the bone', and 'banging wind' may kill 'stubborn hedges'. But the images need to be seen in the context of the dramatic encounter between the victim self and the self that knows about the hawk's powers.

The same is true for many of the best-known poems of the 1950s and 1960s. They are not really about things or animals, but are rather attempts to free oneself from what the 'stare' suggests is unnatural and unreal within oneself. Take the poem 'The Jaguar' (*HR*, p. 12) for example. Here the stare of the crowd at the animal ('the crowd stands, stares, mesmerized') is related to the drowning narrator's role. The stare of the jaguar that hurries 'enraged / Through prison darkness after the drills of his eyes' is the outer observer's or the crowd's perception of a great natural force with which they have no direct contact. This is indicated in the analogy between a child following his dream and a mesmerized crowd following the jaguar. Extrapolating a bit, one can understand the encounter as taking place between civilized man, in reality a 'fallen' natural creature, looking at his own superior self which continues to exist outside him in the jaguar. The animal is above all an energetic being, exploding beyond the bars of his cage like a visionary in his cell. His eyes are drills – blast drills – and his body chases them 'on a short fierce fuse', like a flame stalking dynamite. The animal's stare is a refusal to acknowledge or to be fettered by the external, surface world at all. The eye is 'satisfied to be blind in fire'. This energy exists already, beyond the bars, in the awareness of the mesmerized crowd.

The last six lines of the poem celebrate the jaguar's remarkable perspective by casting off all tokens of sensual imprisonment.

From the speaking voice in the poem, which colludes with the reader – or with the reader's better self – in rejecting the expected causality of the jaguar's 'hurrying enraged' movement, we learn the truth about the animal in the zoo: he does not move out of boredom as we might think, but he 'spins from the bars', since 'there's no cage to him'. In fact,

> The world rolls under the long thrust of his heel.
> Over the cage floor the horizons come.

The jaguar spins the earth under his feet like a ball or a prayer wheel. And, as on a miniature, revolving globe, new lands sweep toward the viewer, blind to the fact that it is he, through the perception of the jaguar, who is moving, and not the earth. Thus the poem moves to a strangely anti-sensory point of view, towards the perspective of the jaguar's otherness. His deafness and blindness to the trivial or low-grade events of the outer world as well as his self-fuelled stare all contribute to his remarkable intensity.

The reader of the poem is forced into a curious position by the internalization that takes place. The radical subjectivity of the jaguar's experience (which lies beyond the senses and almost beyond the imagination) is used to dramatize his power. The metaphors challenge the reader to indentify with a hyperbole which makes the role of the victim in the poem (the witness or the crowd that only half-consciously knows of the jaguar's power) almost invisible. What we are left with is an 'inner' reality and a set of external facts which we can no longer appeal to (the jaguar is *not* what the eye can see, *not* what the ear can hear, etc.).

'The Thought Fox' (*HR*, p. 14) is another well-known poem which deals with the drama of two selves. The first begins as a disembodied imagining ('I imagine this midnight . . .') which takes on life, passing from emptiness to a more sensuous form and finally to words printed on a page. The other self seems virtually to be absent in the first part of the poem until, with something of a shock, we witness the imaginary or imagining 'I' confront a perceiving 'I':

> Till, with a sudden sharp hot stink of fox
> It enters the dark hole of the head.

21

Here the reader must feel a bit unsure of his position. Is he still escorted by the 'I imagine' persona of the first line or are his senses now being assaulted by an imagining that has grown more and more like a fox, sensuous and almost independent? To whom does this 'dark hole of the head' belong? It sounds as if the first narrator is referring to himself now in the third person – to somebody else's head. And the reader needs to shift intuitively to experience both the subjective development of the thought into a fox and its sudden, almost alien, arrival into the conscious mind. The thought creeps up in a way we are now familiar with, as

> an eye,
> A widening deepening greenness . . .
> Coming about its own business . . .

The final lines where we return to the ticking clock but discover now a printed page reveal an external world of time and long-dead imaginings (in print), which feels very distant from the imaginative act, this dark and secret reality of the mind's possession by something akin, in its apartness and its energy, to the jaguar.

The end of another famous anthology piece, 'Pike' (*L*, pp. 56–7), from Hughes's second book, *Lupercal* (1960), again demonstrates clearly the psychodrama which the accusing eye sets in motion. The angler by the monastery pond which is 'as deep as England' and which holds pike 'too immense to stir', dares not cast openly; rather he has cast silently and fished

> With the hair frozen on my head
> For what might move, for what eye might move.

The internalized drama of the staring eye is unavoidable here. Yet the reader's commitment must also be uncertain because of the ambiguity of the phrase 'for what eye might move'. The rephrasing – 'for what might move, for what *eye* might move' – makes us aware of the struggle. Whose eye is this? Is this the eye of the angler, which, unstirring itself, monitors or even contributes to the movement of a fish – *mutatis mutandis*? Or is it the eye of a fish 'out there', which the preternaturally concentrated attention of the angler can pick up, sonar-like. The reader is caught at this point in a moment of inner struggle between the mesmerized stare of the victim, which belongs to the flux of a superficial world, and the fixed, unwavering stare of the accuser, the pike, as it manifests itself in the awareness of the predator-angler. The last verses suggest unequivocally the full psychodrama of possession, conflict and power:

> The still splashes on the dark pond,
>
> Owls hushing the floating woods
> Frail on my ear against the dream
> Darkness beneath night's darkness had freed,
> That rose slowly towards me, watching.

The stare of the 'other' is here a 'dream' which rises from the depths of the cultural and individual unconscious and slowly begins to confront and make insecure the conscious life: the 'darkness beneath night's darkness' has 'freed' it – has freed the pike or the unconscious power within. Thus at the end of the poem we feel that the external world is fading unambiguously away ('Frail on my ear against the dream') while the accusation of the 'other' begins to rise against the would-be predator, the ego.

The poem closes at the beginning of this confrontation. The reader is left trying, through a reflex reaction, to accustom himself to a new kind of perspective, neither objective nor subjective, unlike those which have just been discredited by the power of life beyond the conscious or external world. The reader soon has to realize that the simple distinction between subject and object (or indeed between fisherman and pike or reader and poem) proves here to be quite irrelevant. We are frightened but fascinated witnesses of this seismic disturbance which throws the puny claims and dimensions of waking life into relief and which asserts another reality.

Even in the more celebratory poems of *Wodwo* (1967) which, mantra-like, seem to praise the building blocks of the external sensory world, the reader still meets with the stare and the attendant ambivalence and challenge it provokes by making him supply an inner or a further reality. This is true in 'Skylarks' (*W*, pp. 168–71) for example, where the speaker is straining to pursue the lark with his eye almost to beyond the vanishing point:

>   Dithering in ether
>   Its song whirls faster and faster
>   And the sun whirls
>   The lark is evaporating
>   Till my eye's gossamer snaps
>   and my hearing floats back widely to earth
>   (W, pp. 169–70)

As though tied sensuously to a kite, the gossamer thread tears and lets the lark go free out of earshot. Hughes forces the reader to imagine this even as we imitate the thread and sink back to the earth. We are propelled beyond the sensory limits even as they are asserted.

The prayer-like chant in a poem related to 'Skylarks', 'Gnat-Psalm' (W, pp. 179–81), takes the effect further. Very different in style from the earlier poems referred to above, 'Gnat-Psalm' produces the hypnotic effect of an incantation. The psalm not only celebrates energy but it attempts to dissolve perception itself and exorcise away the body of the staring observer by carrying him (and us) into the dance of atomic particles somewhere near the edge of the troposphere:

>   O little Hasids
>   Ridden to death by your own bodies
>   Riding your bodies to death
>   You are the angels of the only heaven!
>
>   And God is an Almighty Gnat!
>   You are the greatest of all the galaxies!
>   My hands fly in the air, they are follies
>   My tongue hangs up in the leaves
>   My thoughts have crept into crannies
>
>   Your dancing
>
>   Your dancing
>
>   Rolls my staring skull slowly away into outer space.
>   (W, pp. 180–1)

This strange last line, almost like a science fiction fantasy, offers a perilous resolution to the 'stare'. The starer is mesmerized and dismembered and carried off, presumably, to where there are no objects of sight – and thus no sight as we know it. We are left with the challenge to observe from without, as if hearing a confession, or to try to *inhabit* with the speaker the state of objectless staring, filled only with the furious pirouettes of transparent gnats. The gnats lead the eye to the energy of the outside world. But they also serve as a gateway to an inner state where the exterior self and the inner self also dissolve. Our response here depends on how we follow the directional adverb 'away'.

*

So far I have tried to trace the varieties of dramatic encounter which all seem to begin with the evil eye and Scout Rock. This encounter between an ordinary and an extraordinary or revealed self has little in common with the sort of awe felt before Nature's custodial presence seen in Wordsworth's *Prelude*. Though it is difficult to separate the mechanism of the encounter from the specific *message* or nature of the evil eye, it is now worth considering what makes the evil eye or the stare so very powerful psychologically. Does the power of the evil eye come, as Poe argues, from the genius-like, spellbinding void that becomes the frightful thought of what lies beyond experience? From where, if not from such a phantasm, such an idea of a shadow, does the extraordinary self draw its strength?

In answering this question we ask another one: what lies behind Hughes's special sense of the staring eye? Might the feeling of unease relate, not simply to the thought of a non-experience, but to some complicated and powerful fiction or interpretation of nature which has a hold on the poet's mind?

In a story called 'Sunday' (*W*, pp. 56–70) of 1960, Hughes writes about a young boy who goes to a Methodist chapel which is perched on a hill looking out over a valley. Michael's anxieties and fantasies are closely associated with staring eyes and glowering natural presences. On the Sabbath, we are told, the chapel and its 'brainless bells' seem to control the whole valley. 'Life, over the whole countryside, was suspended for the day' (*W*, p. 57). On the one hand the control brings on a retreat into day-dreaming with Michael. He sits in the church thinking of free-ranging wolves, although these mental images are no match for the sermon (*W*, p. 56). On the other hand, the chapel's influence has extended even

25

down to the 'Top Wharf Pub', where a man with 'sparrow-hawk eyes', Billy Red, comes every week to do battle with two rats. He bites them with his own mouth until they screech 'a harsh, ripping, wavering scream' (*W*, p. 66) and die. One Sunday after Church Michael goes down to the pub and witnesses this bizarre spectacle. Like a young lady also present in the crowd of drinkers, Michael is revolted to a point where he feels physically ill and runs away. Yet this revulsion from the barbarism of Billy Red the rat man is complicated. It is related in fact to the young boy's flimsy, day-dream escape from – and yet within – the church's powerful jurisdiction.

Lying like an obstacle both at the centre of Michael's longing for some wild, free natural world and at the heart of his revulsion from Billy Red, is the Methodist chapel. The church truly controls *all* the valley: the pious, the renegade and even evasive thought itself. The chapel has brought about a divorce between dream, idea and imagination on the one hand, and sensual, physical man on the other. The life-hating church has guided the boy in becoming an effete dreamer about creatures long extinct in his valley. It has also caused a group of men to gather like voyeurs around the rat man, so as to confront nature – but at one remove. The church has ushered into the valley a kind of spirituality which excludes body and emasculates mental energy (Michael's dreams). In the rat man it has created a kind of physicality which entirely dispenses with intellect. These two tendencies are but mirror images of one another. Thus when Michael runs off in horror away from Billy Red, it is because, at least intuitively, he has come up against a mental curse, a prohibiting fiction, which he recognizes *as his own* and which has already started him off furtively day-dreaming about wild flesh and energy. At the bottom of both Michael's furtiveness and Billy Red's grossness lies an interpretation of the world which comes from the church. Michael's reaction against Billy Red is not a simple revulsion against some unpleasant external reality (like the precipice of Scout Rock). *External reality has already been deeply influenced by the church*. What Michael really runs away from is not a dramatic manifestation of nature in its primitive or pristine state. He really runs away from the natural world *as it has already been interpreted by the church*.

The consequences of this distinction are important, for we now understand that what Michael truly fears in the rat man's 'sparrow-hawk' eyes is directly related to a prohibition erected by his chapel. The evil eye is not just a dizzying void that excites imaginings of what lies beyond experience but a fictionalized natural world which draws its power to mesmerize *from the sublimation of physical power which a body-hating religion has brought about*. Thus, within the self which perceives the precipice, an earlier, censorious fiction has already made the body and the physical world taboo and thus has effectively split mind and body radically into two opposing realities. For this reason the normal self sees the physical or natural world as something insinuating, monstrous and grotesque.

In a more recent poem written nearly twenty years after 'Sunday', Hughes returns possibly to the same church, here identified as 'Mount Zion', in *Remains of Elmet* (1979; *RE*, p. 82). The poem faces the photograph of a dour, sooty brick chapel. We understand more about why the young boy felt that the precipice beneath Scout Rock or the screech of the rat in Billy Red's animal mouth was being aimed directly *at him*. It was because in the beginning

> Blackness
> Was a building blocking the moon.
> Its wall – my first world-direction –
> Mount Zion's gravestone slab.

In this religion, this 'first direction', the spirit is kept out of the body. As the poem says, Wesleyism represents a noose around the neck. The Word made flesh, according to the Apostle John, has been turned by Mount Zion religion into 'only a naked bleeding worm / Who has given up the ghost'. (This is, by the way, precisely the state of mind Calvin recommends in the *Institutes*.) The Word made flesh has been stripped of its Word and now is a mindless gnawing worm: a terrible, brute nature.

This religion and its effects represent a powerful, destructive force for Hughes. But if, in his poetry, Hughes regrets this religion and campaigns by writing verse to put right its evil doings, he also is oriented by certain deep assumptions of Methodism or radical Protestantism, especially this religion's way of internalizing

27

debate – even when the poet's goal is to put the spirit back into Christ, the 'naked bleeding worm'.

Thus Mount Zion Christianity directs Hughes's quest in more than an adversary way: it gives him as well an astonishing inner certainty and wilfulness. This is manifested typically in the un-usual or preternatural knowledge of what nature and natural energy *really* are, and, hence, what man must strive to emulate (the hawk's eye, the jaguar's stare, the immense pike, the dancing gnat, etc.). The dramatically anti-human knowledge is, I think, associated with a tradition that passes not just through Zwingli, Knox or Calvin, but back to the same conditions of revelation, tragedy and interiorization that characterize the mainspring of the Pietist tradition. If Saul, on the road to Damascus, could see only when blinded by light, so Hughes asserts a visionary's capacity to see things unavailable to ordinary human organs trained to trust sensory impressions and empirical and deductive processes. He sees the powers and motor forces of a Nature-God present invisibly both 'out there' and 'inside', in the mystery of the body itself. This is why casual or familiar forms of knowledge, like autobiographical facts, are suspect when placed before the special awareness of Paul, Saul's superior self. Ironically, in Hughes's world, forces such as Mount Zion, as pervasive and as evil as an intrinsic depravity of human nature itself, are absolutely imposs-ible to dissociate from such familiar kinds of knowledge and facts. Like the church in 'Sunday', these evil forces are a pre-existing reality, a pre-existing fiction, of the natural or external world.

*

Perhaps the idea of mixing censorious Mount Zion with Robert Graves's galvanizing book *The White Goddess* best puts one in mind of the real colour and direction of the poet's emotions and imagination. There can be few more sophisticated and genuinely astounding works (with its effortless synthesis of the whole of Indo-European and Semitic mythologies) than *The White God-dess*. Graves's goal in part is to defend and rehabilitate non-Protestant traditions or traditions inimical to the Protestant point of view. Though most of his book is argued from the perspective of a fervent anti-Protestant, Graves's treatment is so genuinely sophisticated as to appear almost non-sectarian: he blames the

Greeks as well as the Hebrews for the divorce of mind and body (though one may be allowed to imagine that his real quarrel is with the species *Homo sapiens* itself). A key thesis of this key-to-all-mythologies is Graves's analysis of what he calls Greek Olympianism or Socratic 'intellectual homosexuality' (Nietzsche had diagnosed something similar before, in his meditations on late Classical tragedy). The cast of mind, Graves argues, developed in the seventh-century BC Judaism of the prophet Ezekiel. By the fifth century BC, Socrates had fixed the course of our modern rationalist and sceptical culture, for example in his contemptuous dismissal in the *Phaedrus* of Plato's inquiry into the truth or otherwise of the myth of Boreas and Orithya. Puritanism in the early Church and in early modern England represents for Graves a restatement of this anti-mythic, anti-female, brain religion. A long passage is worth quoting since so much of Hughes's outward development – in terms of his own subsequent analysis of Shakespeare, English history and the modern mind – bears Graves's distinctive stamp:

> The result of envisaging this [new] god of pure meditation, the Universal Mind still premised by the most reputable modern philosophers, and enthroning him above Nature as essential Truth and Goodness was not an altogether happy one. Many of the Pythagoreans suffered, like the Jews, from a constant sense of guilt and the ancient poetic Theme [of the White Goddess] reasserted itself perversely. The new God claimed to be dominant as Alpha and Omega, the Beginning and the End, pure Holiness, pure Good, pure Logic, able to exist without the aid of woman; but it was natural to identify him with one of the original rivals of the Theme and to ally the woman and the other rival permanently against him. The outcome was philosophical dualism with all the tragi-comic woes attendant on spiritual dichotomy. If the true God, the God of Logos, was pure thought, pure good, whence came evil and error? The two separate creations had to be assumed: the true spiritual Creation and the false material Creation. (*WG*, p. 465)

A powerful historical and philosophical panorama, indeed, and one that almost immediately elicited a sympathetic response in Hughes's earliest published poem, the 'Song' (*HR*, p. 19), written in 1949 to that dethroned Goddess which Graves describes variously as Isis, mother of the gods, Rhea and her Christian variant, Mary, mother of God. Here is Graves's account of what he calls the Theme, the Goddess in her triple manifestation as Goddess of birth, of life and of death:

> The Goddess is a lovely, slender woman with a hooked nose, deathly pale face, lips red as rowan-berries, startlingly blue eyes and long fair hair; she will suddenly transform herself into sow, mare, bitch, vixen. . . . Her names and titles are innumerable. In ghost stories she often figures as 'The White Lady', and in ancient religions, from the British Isles to the Caucasus, as the 'White Goddess'. . . . The reason why the hairs stand on end, the eyes water, the throat is constricted, the skin crawls and a shiver runs down the spine when one writes or reads a true poem is that a true poem is necessarily an invocation of the White Goddess, or Muse, the Mother of All Living, the ancient power of fright and lust – the female spider or the queen-bee whose embrace is death. (*WG*, p. 24)

Moreover, the true poet 'is in love with the White Goddess, with Truth: his hearth breaks with longing and love for her' (*WG*, p. 448).

This is precisely the Lady whom Hughes addresses in his 'Song'. But note how *inaccessible* she is:

> You stood, and your shadow was my place:
> You turned, your shadow turned to ice . . .

Note the *indignation* felt towards the men who have defiled the Lady:

> Since my heart heard [your music] and all to pieces fell
> Which your lovers stole, meaning ill . . .

Finally note the revenge that *Nature* (with which a poet, 'worn out with love', is intimately associated) will take in sorting out the corrupt world of brash men and the physical/spiritual dichotomy they cause. It will be a revenge to vindicate the poet's frustrated love for the Lady. Most astonishingly, this revenge will take place only *after the poet's death*, when the head has finally turned into dust and has submitted itself to the Lady's sovereignty.

30

The whole poem is addressed to the Lady, in each stanza, but the real subject is the encounter between evil men, with whom the poet is indirectly associated through his own mental existence, and the Lady Nature, with whom another part of the poet is associated, in the form of the assenting or indeed inciting participant in the Lady's revenge. In this way, and in a minor key perhaps, the poem can be read as an expiation of guilt through self-imposed tragedy, the triumph of Lady Nature over the man/mind in death. This is, again, another variant on Hughes's account of the mountaineer who has to scale his mountain to rid himself of the curse of the sheer cliff's eye.

Thus from 1949, when 'Song' was written, up to the present day, most of Hughes's work is structured like this poem (the plangent Gravesian aubade is quite exceptional – Hughes's women tend to be ferocious, energetic creatures, like his 'Hawk Roosting', *L*, p. 26). Almost always we see a dialogue between a superior person, who takes on the mantle of all-knowing Nature, and a lesser, more human person, who feels guilty or accused of some fundamental transgression. In a way, one could say that all of Ted Hughes's poetry is a variation on the Dr Jekyll and Mr Hyde theme, with this twist: Hyde, the body and repulsive toad, is the real possessor of knowledge, and Jekyll, the enlightened or sophisticated mind, is the guilt-ridden, accused party. We often feel that this debate takes place before yet another party, who identifies with both men, and participates through them, as through an advocate and a solicitor, to rid himself of the Jekyll curse. This third party we sense is the poet himself or, from the reader's point of view, a kind of guiding spirit who sets the dialogue moving.

*

Certainly Saul on the road to Damascus knew where he got his special insight from, and it may be otiose to wonder where Ted Hughes gets his special insight or revelation from. But it is, I think, worth quoting a few passages which show how Hughes himself finds support for his insight in the more objectified world of science and anthropology. This expression of beliefs, in a more public or conventional idiom, gives us some external emblems of the myth or insight which the poet in countless ways refers back to. In this limited sense we can understand where his beliefs come from, from the way they flesh themselves out as evidence in the following choice of passages:

Our six senses, which are the essential meaning-finders for our practical existence, have become somewhat stupefied. We have lost touch with certain useful instincts. Our inter-bred, laboratory-coddled wits, displaced by automata from their essential services, grow more and meaninglessly theoretical, more and more passive and infantile. Our brain case shrinks, our thyroid glands are going to sleep, our adrenal glands are withering, and our sexual organs and interests tyrannize over a vast psychic idleness or a swarm of neurotic ailments (Review of *The Nerve of Some Animals* and *Man and Dolphin*, *New Statesman*, 23 March 1962). Poetry at its most primitive seems first to occur as a one-line chant of nonsense syllables in accompaniment to the rhythm of a stamping dance. Chimpanzees have got this far, and with them there is evidently not much before it (Review of *Primitive Song*, *The Listener*, 3 May 1962). The word 'rationality' is having a bad time. The laws of the Creation are the only literally rational things, and we don't yet know what they are. The nearest we can come to rational thinking is to stand respectfully, hat in hand, before this Creation, exceedingly alert for a new word. We no longer so readily make the grinding, funicular flight of cerebrations from supposed first principles (Review of *Astrology* and *Ghost and Diving-rod*, *New Statesman*, 2 October 1964). The deeper into language one goes, the less visual/conceptual its imagery, and the more audial/visceral/muscular its system of tensions. This accords with the biological fact that the visual nerves connect with the modern human brain, while the audial nerves connect with the cerebellum, the primal animal brain and nervous system, direct. In other words, the deeper into language one goes, the more dominated it becomes by purely musical modes, and the more dramatic it becomes – the more unified with total states of being and with the expressiveness of physical action. Visualization in language is at odds with immediately expressive dramatic action in that it is the conceptual substitute for physical action (*Orghast*, p. 45; notes given by Hughes to A. C. H. Smith).

32

The tenor of this collage of remarks made between 1962 and 1971 is strikingly similar, even if the topics vary a good deal. One can see the extent to which Hughes borrows from Graves while shifting the emphasis away from cultural history to evolutionary history. Thus, instead of Graves's ogres – Socrates, Ezekiel, Calvin and Cromwell – we see, with Hughes, the demon of human frontal lobes, the evolutionary development which separates us from the rest of the animal kingdom.

From the perspective of the poetry, all these quotations relate to the superior eye, the extraordinary awareness, whose origins Hughes traces back to some pre-human animal and his ancient sensual-sympathetic nervous system, upon which a new system has perversely grown. What is perhaps most typical of Hughes's perspective is the way in which elements of Mount Zion religion have recrudesced in a naturalistic form. Instead of man's Fall through experience, the Tree of Knowledge, and the redeeming God of revelation, we have man's 'psychic idleness' and the extraordinary truth of a 'primal animal brain and nervous system'. However much Graves's teachings on poetry, mythology and history may have oriented Hughes's own readings in archaeology and ethnology, the basic structure of his values returns in all these quotations to those tensions established very early on by a certain church in a certain valley, of whose influence the 'evil cliff' of Scout Rock is a first witness. Although Hughes reverses nominally the elements of Mount Zion fiction – Nature for God, and experience for innocence, the role of revelation in both is constant. The Mount Zion tradition calls it enthusiasm or visible sainthood. Hughes calls the same 'the bigger energy, the elemental power circuit of the Universe' (Interview I, p. 9), the power that becomes available if one lives close to the older nervous system.

*

In his early works, Hughes dramatizes the conflict between the visual/conceptual self and the audial/visceral self he refers to above. This process is not simple because each poem sets out new conditions for the conflict, and thus illuminates a different aspect of the central myth. The act of writing verse itself brings together, usually in a frail, momentary narrative or a climactic conceit, these opposed perspectives, and presents the reader with a

33

challenge. What position shall one take in relation to the conflict between the two audible voices, the one which does not comprehend the meaning of the hawk's eye, and the other which does? The poet is silent, apparently refusing to mediate. And yet he is the source of the struggle we perceive in the poem. Only indirectly and implicitly (for us readers) does the poet, after, or in the course of the struggle, become active as a healer or as what one could call a myth-maker. The activity of this myth-maker, as we will see, is the reason why, according to Hughes, poetry exists at all.

2

MYTH AND HUGHES'S CONTEXT

Objectively or rationally, myth may be looked upon as archaic superstition. Every poet, whether Romantic and subjective or Classical and objective, is none the less a myth-maker, a person who renames the world by reordering familiar words or making new ones. Stringing sounds — words with new meanings — together, one articulates mythic utterances in the form of a story, a verbal gesture or a drama. In the previous chapter I spoke of a second or implied narrator in 'The Hawk in the Rain', whose job it was to bring together the extraordinary experience of the hawk's eye and the drowning man in the ploughland. The implied narrator, the presence we may identify with the poet's own, has a mythic task in the sense that, behind the poem or through the poem, he is making a gesture that will bridge Nature's ineffable power and the weakness of the plodding man (the person the reader initially accepts as the narrator of the poem but who turns out to be the lesser half of the real or superior self objectified in the hawk's eye). In this way, both mythic naming and mythic narrative in Hughes aim to join man and experience, reader and poem, and to challenge, accommodate, or heal, the sense of exclusion provoked by the hawk's eye.

Here are two quotations in which Hughes explains his own sense of myth and the purpose of poetry. The first is from 1976, the second from 1970.

Objective imagination, in the light of science, rejected religion as charlatanism, and the inner world as a bundle of fairy tales, a relic of primeval superstition. . . . Religious negotiations had formerly embraced and humanized the archaic energies of instinct and feeling. They had conversed in simple but profound terms with the forces struggling inside people, and had civilized them, or attempted to. Without religion, those powers have become dehumanized. The whole inner world has become elemental, chaotic, continually more primitive and beyond our control. (Myth II, p. 90)

The assertions here are, of course, debatable. Science in itself is no less mythic in its origins than poetry. What seems to matter most for Hughes, however, is that our grip on these origins – on the basic stories or hypotheses that move science – has grown rigid or dogmatic. What results is a culture out of touch with Nature, or in touch with Her in only a very narrow way: thus Nature becomes, beyond this narrow conception, elemental, chaotic and dangerous. In a sense, this is how Nature appears through the hawk's eye. Now, asks Hughes, how does one respond?

A mentally sick person is sick, says [Freud's] theory, because there is something in his mind which he refuses to face, which he has by some means or other cut himself off from and which he represses into the cellars of his mind, down into the nervous system where it plays havoc. And this devil of suppressed life stops making trouble the moment he is acknowledged, the moment he is welcomed into conscious life and given some shape where he can play out his energy in an active part of the personality. The best way to welcome him and to release him, it is reckoned, is within the framework of a fantasy. Once the fantasy has made connection with the demon and given him a role, the person feels cured. (Myth I, p. 58)

In this way, telling stories, writing poems or fantasizing performs the mythic function of taming a devil, for example the devil of the hawk's eye. Myth, then, is the objectified story of a psychic healing, a taming of the dragon, a coming-to-terms-with drama. As tragedy, myth aims to expel or accommodate some evil: the curse of Thebes, centered upon the riddle of the sphinx, the alienation of mind and body, the stare of Nature, or, as in the ever-popular space film, some enemy from another planet – some new monster for a Saint George. The poet, according to Hughes, is the healer of the community as well as of himself, a medicine man, a marabout, a shaman:

> You choose a subject because it serves, because you *need* it. We go on writing poems because one poem never gets the whole account right. There is always something missed. At the end of the ritual up comes a goblin. (Interview I, p. 15; my emphasis)

The poem sets out to resolve the poet's or the community's ill. Thus myth is not only a making or a renewing of the old world. Subjectively, the making itself is also therapeutic, in a deep and immemorial sense as well as an everyday, practical sense.

To illustrate this point it is perhaps best to look straight away at a clear example of the myth-maker at work. The example that serves best here is one of Hughes's most popular books for children (over 150,000 copies sold in the UK alone), *The Iron Man* (1968). The work tells a kind of St George and the Dragon story, though in a form more akin to the invader-from-outer-space Hollywood B movie of the 1950s.

Hughes's intruder is a giant Iron Man who crashes to earth one day. All the metal parts of his body are broken up. The Iron Man begins however to put himself back together, scavenging for metal around near-by farms, eating a tractor here and an automobile there. At first young Hogarth, who has discovered the monster, calls out to the farmers of the community to try to destroy the Iron Man. The farmers try to bury him by luring him into an earth trap. But the Iron Man escapes. Hogarth then has a good idea and persuades people to make friends with the Iron Man by allowing him to live in a scrap metal dump. Thus, the Iron Man becomes integrated ecologically into the English country town.

But then a 'space-bat-angel-dragon' suddenly falls from a distant star on to the earth, covering up the whole of Australia. Immediately the two outsiders are involved in a test of strength to determine who can endure the hottest flames. Helped by humans (with vague technological connections), the Iron Man lets himself be roasted. Then, as agreed, his opponent flies back to his star to undergo a similar trial by fire. The battle rages until the Iron Man wins. Yet, instead of destroying *his* threatening invader, the 'space-bat-angel-dragon', the Iron Man transforms him (with his consent) into the music of the spheres, a sort of humming, inter-galactic glue. In the end both androids become important parts of the human world, and, through them, humans can participate in the cohesive and energetic forces of the cosmos.

It is worth quoting from what Hughes himself says about the old myth he has just remade:

> If I had been concerned to write an ordinary monster story, I would have had my little boy destroy the Iron Man, maybe, in the first episode. . . . In psychoanalytical terms, for there are no others that you can really use, he enters [at the point of meeting the monster] into a sort of neurotic condition. In other words, a terror has arrived and the only way he can deal with the terror is by pushing it underground. (Myth I, p. 65)

But this, Hughes says, would be to commit a crime – not only against the Iron Man but against ourselves. Thus when the monster re-emerges, one has to face the crime and not make the same mistake again. Hogarth shows the others the right way to deal with the alien, though their first instinct is to restore the status quo at any cost. No 'intrusions from the unknown' for them. They are determined to avoid the great energies of space. But, in Hughes's story, this is quite impossible. The energy is a reality which cannot be overlooked or buried in the subconscious.

As for the boy hero, he manages to bring the dragon into his world. He serves as a model of one who keeps his contacts with the whole outer world open and unimpeded. The monster henceforth will be a force for the good, and a source of renewed human vigour. Thus, through a simple story, well known in its many forms to all in our culture, Hughes attempts to bring together ordinary, waking man (Hogarth and the farmers who wish first of all to defend the status quo) with the extraordinary reality of astral energy. As Hughes comments, this operation is essentially a psychological one, since we – the poet himself and we the readers – are simultaneously farmer, little boy and dragon from outer space, at once ordinary self attached to a familiar world and an extraordinary self, visited by energies way beyond what the former self can understand. When we refuse the dragon, as Hughes emphasizes, we commit a crime against ourselves: the energy out there *is* real. It 'can't be ignored . . . they can't push it away; it's just too powerful and obtrusive. It's come a bit too near' (Myth I, p. 65).

Here it is clear what myth is supposed to achieve. The two selves seen throughout the discussion of 'The Hawk in the Rain', 'The Jaguar' and the other early poems in the previous chapter are supposed to merge or become unified through the telling of stories or the writing of poems. And the reader, identifying with the process, is brought to utter, with the poet, 'I *am* this otherness' and 'it *is* me'. Alien world and self, inferior and superior selves – all join as we are led to accept the monstrous power from 'outer space', or, indeed, inner space. As the angel part of the dragon's name suggests, the new power will ultimately become the very source of a deeper, cosmic unity – that music of space, the energetic principle of harmony which exerts its full force in the apotheosis at the end of *The Iron Man*. (From a much more subjective point of view, the same apotheosis is repeated at the end of 'Skylarks' and 'Gnat-Psalm'.)

*

The knowledge that the dragon will not go away is the same knowledge that confronts the drowning narrator in 'The Hawk in the Rain'. Its cognition depends itself on a special insight, perhaps like a hallucination or, in terms of ordinary sensory data, some revelation of a supersensible quality. Incarnating this revelation is directly or indirectly the imperative which a poem or story seeks to address. The real God, Nature, behind this knowledge and opposite the ordinary mind, has the same feel about Him and the same requirements for salvation as the non-Hellenized, Old Testament or Protestant God. The only difference is that He carries the name Nature, and rational man that of wayward or depraved creation. (Hughes, as seen, prefers to explain this naturalistically as a kind of evolutionary mishap.) Like the radical God of Pietism, the God Nature is part and parcel of an existential or inner tragedy, quite different in feel from the 'outer' tragedy, which involves recognition of man's separateness from an Apollonian order, as in the case of Oedipus the King. Hughes's God – like Abraham's, or that of Milton's *Samson Agonistes* – must ultimately speak to man mythically. 'I *am* the Almighty God; walk before me and be thou perfect' (Gen. 17:1). Seen from man's

39

perspective (the pre-covenant or lesser man Abram, later to be renamed Abraham), the revelation of God is a tragedy that brings on a continuous effort to incarnate Him, to live His Word out in deed, for example in the making of poetry. This is what the implied narrator behind the speaking voices, the poet himself, is doing in 'The Hawk in the Rain'. This is specifically what Hughes says he is doing in *The Iron Man*. But, objectively, the task is absurd: it never ends, just as revelations from some greater God are bound never to end. (The Bible objectifies this narration.) This is to say that, subjectively, there is no apotheosis, no golden harmony, at the end of *The Iron Man*, any more than God's covenant with Abraham in the Bible settles things once and for all. Tragedy – that recurring awareness of a smaller self and a bigger, more enlightened self – is itself a perpetual condition, both for the Christian plodder and for Hughes's ever-returning inferior self who is intimidated by the staring eye. The prayer at the end of 'Gnat-Psalm' or the astral music at the end of *The Iron Man* are both aspects – the one expressive and subjective, the other objectified by narrative – of the mind's way of imitating the arch hero of Christian tragedy, the character who keeps trying and trying and trying – like Bunyan's plodding Christian or Albert Camus's (very un-Greek) Sisyphus, in his *Mythe de Sisyphe*.

Damned to a repetitive and objectively pointless task, this man not only developed some powerful muscles but (according to Camus) also began actually to enjoy the scenery and even the contour of his odious rock. For Hughes as well, to look at what one is doing objectively is to slip into the curse itself of our lesser 'I', dominated as it is by an ineffectual brain wedded to surface reality. For Hughes this is the trap. For Bunyan, the same danger is objectified in the many forces and thoughts which pop up to taunt Christian. For Stevenson, the same trap was symbolized in the growing tyranny of Hyde over Jekyll. The great danger in all four men's work is the seductive consciousness of the self as object. However expressed, the result is that one is cut off from and made to forswear the other self that is aware of God.

As Hughes says above: after the ritual another goblin always appears, i.e. another poem has to be begun. This is, in a practical sense, what I mean by Hughes's Christian-like response to revelation, as a radical subject who is determined to incarnate his special insights through unceasing myth-making. From this (subjective) perspective, there is no goal really, no New Jerusalem. For Hughes, as for the radical Protestant or the philosopher of the 'absurd', this New Jerusalem is an ever-receding, ever-changing goblin. From the only point of view that really matters – the one that is focused on the world of energy – for much of Hughes's career, what is important in terms of man's quest for God is not the arrival 'there', but rather the journey hence.

*

The nature of Hughes's God and the radical subjectivity of his perspective distinguish his from temperaments that are content to rely on reason and normal faculties, from those which feel God or ultimate value to lie just 'under the surface' of things, in immanence. For Hughes, ordinary sensory perceptions are of small value compared, say, to the vision of the hawk as revealed in a roosting hawk's drowsy meditations:

> I sit in the top of the wood, my eyes closed . . .

> There is no sophistry in my body:
> My manners are tearing off heads –

> The allotment of death. (*L*, p. 26)

Like the jaguar already seen, the inside of the hawk is a perfect replica of the outer, active predator. Thought and action are aspects of one incredibly energetic being. Likewise, the otter's superhuman greatness comes from the ability to move freely through, thus connecting, the main zones of the earth: into the air it breathes, upon the land and into the fresh or salt water:

> Oil of water body, neither fish nor beast . . .
> Four-legged yet water-gifted, to outfish fish;   (*L*, p. 46)

and this is because of his 'slippery power' which eludes the keenest of human stalkers. Like so many other animals, the otter is invisible to ordinary man and unknowable to the senses:

> So the self under the eye lies,
> Attendant and withdrawn. (*L*, p. 47)

41

The pike as well has outwitted and outlived human meanings. It belongs to the 'legendary depths', and, over the years, has displayed more resilience than the religious order which 'planted' it. Around the pond where the pike lurks, we are told that mere lilies and muscular tench have 'outlasted every visible stone' placed to hold in the water. Similarly, in another poem, 'Thrushes' (L, p. 52), we are told that the visible bird is belied by some deeper, unfathomable meaning:

> a poised
> Dark deadly eye, those delicate legs
> Triggered to stirrings beyond sense . . . (L, p. 52)

Rarely we see the truth in another human being. But whether we could possibly understand it seems doubtful. Here is Dick Straightup, a human cousin of the thrush or the pike:

> To be understood
> His words must tug up the bottom-most stones of this village,
> This clutter of blackstone gulleys, peeping curtains,
> And a graveyard bigger and deeper than the village
> That sways in the tide of wind and rain some fifty
> Miles off the Irish sea. . . .
>
> His upright walk,
> His strong back, I commemorate now,
> And his white blown head going out between a sky and an
>   earth
> That were bundled into placeless blackness, the one
> Company of his mind. ('Dick Straightup', L, p. 18)

Dick Straightup, like the otter, links the dead with the living and with the gods. He is a human ygdrasil or holy ash linking the main zones of the world ('white blown head going out between a sky and an earth'), and when he speaks, he uses words like the thrush, that go way back to the origins of the village or of man himself. For us, this head and its words are beyond sense, too. They belong to 'placeless blackness'.

One can say generally that Hughes's mood, as seen in several manifestations above, is opposed to pantheism. His God is much

42

too unavailable to be scattered here and there, ready for the careful feel or look. Though subjective, Hughes is totally opposed to idealism, to the point of view that says truth is concerned above all with the powers of the mind, imaginative or rational. Truthful insights, as far as Hughes is concerned, are simply the content of true experience. For him the process of self-consciously making a reader aware of the medium of words and symbols would be a betrayal of that content. A casual remark about Sylvia Plath's and his own reading of poetry in the late 1950s is especially revealing:

> But all along, though with a growing scepticism, she preserved her admiration for Wallace Stevens. He was a kind of god to her, while I could never see anything at all in him except magniloquence. . . . By contrast, I was infatuated with John Crowe Ransom when I first met her [Plath], and I brought her into that infatuation as well. . . . His is not a world you can explore for ever and ever. But his best poems are very final objects. (Interview II, pp. 210–11)

One can appreciate Hughes's early attraction to the densely woven fabric of the work of John Crowe Ransom, the American Southern poet and New Critic – of poems like 'Antique Harvesters' or 'Painted Head' – without really being able to detect similarities that matter. But what he says about Wallace Stevens is much more interesting. Whether he is talking about Stevens the imagist or Stevens the symbolist, both are lost to him by an excessive attention to verbal games or 'magniloquence'. Above, in 'Thrushes', Hughes claims to put 'stirrings beyond sense' into language. This language either rises to the challenge of such extraordinary meanings as the thrush's stirrings or it does not. For Hughes, figures of speech always have their primary meaning in what he refers to as 'audial/visceral', primary man, from which a 'visual/conceptual' man has grown estranged. For Hughes, successful figures of speech give the literal meaning, the real content of *true* experience. The surface meaning of metaphors thus belongs to unreal man and his unreal (visual/conceptual) experience, and are therefore expendable as are our surface impressions.

Yet what Hughes calls 'magniloquence' is precisely the hallmark of a totally different kind of poet – visual and ideal – and of the different means by which he makes us aware of the unknown perspective, of a blackbird or of a jar in Tennessee. The difference is striking if one recalls Hughes's attitude to language when reading from Stevens's 'On the Manner of Addressing Clouds' for example, where the act of growing aware of the metaphor and of being able to change it gives to language, for both poet and reader, an autonomy over experience which Hughes would find symptomatic of the depravity of the brain and its favourite gew-gaws, words: playfully grandiose, Stevens praises 'funest philosophers' whose evocations 'are the speech of clouds', i.e. both ideal and insubstantial. Yet these words, these symbols, are all that one has, if, in the flux of the world,

> You are to be accompanied by more
> Than mute, bare splendors of the sun and moon.

In his essay 'Imagination as Value', Stevens says 'Imagination is the power of mind over the possibilities of things.' Hughes might respond: 'The possibilities of things depend on the imagination's submission to them.'

A complementary point could be made by comparing Hughes's 'Skylarks', discussed in the previous chapter, with Shelley's famous 'blithe spirit! / Bird thou never wert . . . unembodied joy . . . Like a Poet hidden / In the light of thought'. Shelley praises physical absence, the invisible bird whose song brings alive the heavens of the poet's free-flying imagination. For Hughes, the task is to submit the mind, through something like a trance or an hallucination, to the physiological creature, climbing, gasping, dithering in ether, heart drumming like a motor. Until the mind of the reader passes fully into the energy of the bird and its 'conscience perfect', the animal does not really exist – *because* it has come to rest in the mind as an idea. The energetic bird, Hughes would say, is ultimately the exact counter of the word 'skylark'. Stated the other away around, 'skylark' *is* the adequate figure of speech for the energetic animal, as long as that figure of speech is, as it were, experienced rather than understood. For Shelley the bird's near non-existence is a condition of asserting the mind's high-flying reality, and, as a metaphor, the bird's essential reality only becomes apparent when the word that describes the physical animal becomes transparent or invisible, when we grow aware that the bird really *is* a disembodied sound.

Taking the contrast further, it is interesting to compare Gerard Manley Hopkins's poem 'The Windhover' with 'The Hawk in the Rain' which it superficially resembles. The feel of the two poems is polar: in the one, God is humanized not only in the Christ/bird/court imagery but in the way this mainly visual imagery suffices to translate Him into a gnostic and moral human reality. With Hughes, God, as focused in the eye of the hawk, is above all hidden, accessible for the briefest of moments and then only when man is least like his normal self, either drowning or hallucinating. The power behind the hawk is hostile to the ordinary senses. Hopkins *sees* Jesus, God's Word made Flesh, in 'daylight's dauphin'. The sensuous reality of the creature – 'wimpling wing', sweeping 'smooth on a bow-bend', then gliding and rebuffed – joined with its rhythmic translation into the poem and enlarged by the noble but not unhuman ethical imagery of chivalry, brings the invisible straight into the world of ordinary vision and recognizable moral codes. The awful, brute beauty of the falcon, both herald and coming Christ, is even more approachable through the images of the plodding plough, which achieves the same colour as the bird through humdrum, repetitive use, and the near-extinct ember whose secret centre reveals an analogous colour, 'gold-vermilion'. Hopkins explains the coming Word made flesh directly to the senses and through the moral and social metaphors of courtliness and honest ploughing. By contrast, Hughes's bird is accusing, insinuating and inaccessible. The pike, who knows secrets the monks never could have guessed at, stares, 'as a vice locks' (just after gulping down one of his brothers). Where Hopkins, by making his symbolic falcon available to eye and to ear, underscores the closeness of man, Nature and God, Hughes tends, in the early verse at least, to emphasize the contrary: the distance between man and Nature and, indeed, the treachery of sensuous translations of God into symbols, descriptions and words. For example, the hawk roosting has no 'sophistry' in *its* body and, unlike garrulous *Homo sapiens*, needs no arguments to assert its right: this is because, for the hawk, God himself – the sun – is behind him (L, p. 26). Similarly, gnat language – 'their crazy lexicon . . . their dumb Cabala' (W, p. 179) – has everything a human language does not have, because it is a pure body language, the eloquent dance of God's tiniest particle, before which all human symbols, even words, become, like their schizoid interpreters, half mind (meaning) and half body (sound).

*

In terms of the traditions of English poetry Hughes has been compared to the first of the Romantic 'Nature-poets', Wordsworth, author of the 'Immortality' ode and of the *Prelude*. I have already drawn a distinction in the previous chapter, but generally what sets Hughes apart is the absence of a direct, sensuous link with God. In place of Wordsworth's salutary images and recollections of childhood:

> Behold the Child . . .
>
> Thou, whose exterior semblance doth belie
>   Thy Soul's immensity;
> Thou best Philosopher who yet dost keep
> Thy heritage, thou Eye among the blind . . .
>
>   Mighty Prophet! Seer blest!
>   ('Ode: Intimations of Immortality', st. 7, 8)

one can see a much more tortuous path leading to the natural state or to true experience. In 'The Man Seeking Experience Enquires his Way of a Drop of Water', true experience, the drop of water itself, is likened to a child. But this child's message is quite intimidating. The drop of water

> . . . no more responded than the hour-old child
>
> . . . who lies long, long and frowningly
> Unconscious under the shock of its own quick
> After that first alone-in-creation cry
> When into the mesh of sense, out of the dark,
> Blundered the world-shouldering monstrous 'I'.
>
>   (*HR*, pp. 37–8)

In the adult mind the child's state of mind is like that achieved in prayer, a 'numbness', 'an unconscious kind of consciousness' (NT). But such conditions of well-being are elusive and Hughes finds himself being for ever brought back to the Sisyphean or radically subjective solution of continuous tragedy and remaking

46

– back to the recurring engagement with the troubling stare of Natural experience which requires each time a fresh, mythic or healing response.

If Hughes's extraordinary insights into Nature constitute, as vision, the content that determines and directs his poetic and moral forms (such as the inner drama), then one should perhaps cite William Blake among Hughes's predecessors, and especially the extraordinary visions that gave rise to the Prophetic Books. For this comparison, though, allowance must be made for Blake's anti-naturalism, or, more precisely, his anti-deism. Still, his original, primal man, Albion, is not greatly different from Hughes's man in touch with the ancient nervous system. By contrast, however, Hughes has only once attempted the sort of objectification of his vision (in *Gaudete*) that is found as relatively stable allegory in Blake. By the same token, it is rather testing to imagine how Hughes, like another writer with a visionary side, Yeats, would 'sort it all out' in a book like *A Vision*. Hughes has done something like this in private and in his notes for the play *Orghast*. Again, it is remarkable how much ordinary, sensuous reality is struck out by Hughes (where in Yeats, for example, we have the analogies of different kinds of temperament, phases of the moon and so on). Indeed it seems to me that Blake's 'Tyger' or Yeats's 'The Second Coming' are relatively less privileged sorts of vision than, say, 'The Jaguar' (*HR*, p. 12) or 'Second Glance at a Jaguar' (*W*, pp. 25–6). Astounded by the tiger, Blake wants to know who could, who *dared* make it. Yeats is clearly horrified by the imminent arrival of a totally new, totally subjective era of passionate intensity: he knows it runs counter to a 'ceremony of innocence'; and yet, with what has the feel of deep ambivalence, he assents to the changing wheel of fate, as an antithetical self, in the form of the rough beast of the horizon.

The creature in 'Second Glance at a Jaguar' appears sovereign by contrast, Hughes's relationship to it being intimated only in the mantra which *it* mutters:

> His head
> Is like the worn down stump of another whole jaguar,
> His body is just the engine shoving it forward,
> Lifting the air up and shoving on under,

> The weight of his fangs hanging the mouth open,
> Bottom jaw combing the ground. . . .
> Muttering some mantrah, some drum-song of murder
> To keep his rage brightening . . . (W, p. 25)

Blake is astonished, Yeats is revolted but curious; Hughes gives us, above all, the imperious, untouchable creature. Only through the most radical of subjective responses can one have a rapport with Hughes's animal (compared to the relatively humanized subjectivity of Blake's shock and Yeats's revulsion/attraction): this is hinted at in the mantra, the state of self-mesmerization wherein the ordinary waking mind, the exterior, sensory being, is wiped out and the sympathetic nervous system takes over. In this sort of state, Hughes suggests, one gets near God, the ultimate value of the energy that brims in the jaguar. About the jaguar, Hughes told Egbert Faas:

> I prefer to think of [the poem] as first [a] description of a jaguar, second . . . [an] invocation of the Goddess, third . . . [an] invocation of a jaguar-like body of elemental force, demonic force. . . . A jaguar after all can be received in several different aspects . . . he is a beautiful, powerful nature spirit, he is a homicidal maniac, he is a supercharged piece of cosmic machinery, he is a symbol of man's baser nature shoved down into the id and growing cannibal murderous with deprivation, he is an ancient symbol of Dionysus since he is a leopard raised to the ninth power, he is a precise historical symbol to the bloody-minded Aztecs and so on. Or he is simply a demon . . . a lump of ectoplasm. A lump of astral energy. (Interview I, p. 8)

Knowing how dispossessed of this 'astral energy' Hughes feels man to be ('nature shoved down into the id' that grows 'cannibal murderous with deprivation' is a violent development of the incipient sublimation and neurosis Hughes described in *The Iron Man*), and recalling 'invocation' as the word that describes *his* relation to the jaguar, one must be impressed by the radical subjectivity required to become intimate with this emissary of highest value. 'Invocation' is another word for prayer or charm, which is what the poet (or the surprised reader of 'Second Glance

48

at a Jaguar') is supposed to agree to utter *himself* if he is ever going to identify or understand this superior self, the powerful jaguar.

If I underscore this subjectivity in Hughes, compared to Blake or Yeats, it is only by way of expressing through comparison what I feel the real tenor of Hughes's works to be. Others may indeed admire 'Second Glance at a Jaguar' as a fine description of the animal in motion, and it is this; others may say it is an allegory of nature in our scientific era, and this is certainly also true. But, for my part, I feel that what is most signal about this poem, and what gives nearly all of Hughes's writings their specific quality, is the relationship the poet or silent narrator subtly develops between himself, the spectator, and his visionary *alter ego*, who is both part of the spectator and part of the jaguar. It is the drama inherent in this meeting which matters most in Hughes's poetry.

*

Given this analysis, or, less contentiously, what Hughes says about his own poetry, it is hardly surprising that critics have rarely done more than underscore the great gulf that exists between Hughes and the poets of the 'Movement': Kingsley Amis (b. 1922), Donald Davie (b. 1922), D. J. Enright (b. 1920), Philip Larkin (b. 1922) or John Wain (b. 1925), among others. Davie, the leading critical light of the group, has made a point on several occasions, in *Purity of Diction in English Verse* (1952), *Articulate Energy* (1957) and *Thomas Hardy and British Poetry* (1973), of arguing for the centrality and the great value of plain talk in English poetry, from the late-Augustan lucidity of Wesley's hymns to the worthiness of Thomas Hardy as a model for contemporary verse. Davie opposes, at the same time, the centre-stage roles assigned to Yeats, Pound and Eliot, thus asserting both an essential 'Englishness' and an ancestral nobility in opting for the low-key approach.

Hughes has rarely struck out at other writers, but he has made devasting remarks about the poetry of the 'Movement' first collected in the *New Lines* anthology of 1956. What Hughes says does also remind us that he belongs to a basically different generation from that of the 'Movement', to the generation of 'angry young men' (John Osborne (b. 1929)) or of Harold Pinter's (b. 1930) new theatre, to a generation of artists who lived the war vicariously, and thus had a different feeling for energy. On the other hand, the poets of the 'Movement' had seen the Second World War

> turn into death camps and atomic bombs. All they wanted was to get back into civvies and get home to the wife and kids and for the rest of their lives not a thing was going to interfere with a nice cigarette and a nice view of the park. . . . [The war] set them dead against negotiation with anything outside the cosiest arrangement of society. . . . Now I came a bit later. I hadn't had enough. I was all for opening negotiations with whatever happened to be out there. It's just as with the hawk. Where I conjured up a jaguar, they smelt a storm-trooper. (Interview I, pp. 10–11)

Yet, despite all the real and strategic attitudes to be found amongst the 'Movement' poets – the best-known being Larkin's 'I remember, I remember' or Amis's 'Against Romanticism' – the distance between Hughes and Davie, I think, is not quite as vast as most people have assumed. The difference between Hughes and Larkin is quite different from that which is frequently supposed.

Hughes and Davie are both fundamentally poets of experience, both opposed to the idealism of a Stevens, a Yeats or an Ashbery. When Larkin sloughs off his small-town stoicism, he can appear to be in possession of a vision as mammoth and as mystical as Hughes's is mammoth and overwhelming, such as the 'High Windows' thought of 'sun comprehending glass, / And beyond it, the deep blue air, that shows / Nothing, and is nowhere, and is endless'. This may represent a mirror to the mind, disabused of the illusory paradise one generation sees in the other's activities, or it may just be a way of flipping out of the grey world of fucking and harvesting. Still, if Larkin does answer the pointless generation he witnesses, it is with an image of absent endlessness which is also full of energy ('sun comprehending glass'), an image not too distant from the *staggering presence* Hughes no doubt would have invoked in its place.

Comparing Hughes to Davie, in one of the latter's best poems, 'With the Grain' (1957), one finds more proximity than might be supposed – especially given the comments Davie has made about Hughes's and Graves's adherence to 'mythological Never-Never

50

lands'. 'With the Grain' is a quest for a pure, mythic language not unlike that which Hughes invokes in his 'Gnat-Psalm'. True, the rapport between the poet and this ideal language strikes one as being less fraught with tragedy and dying-to-the-old-self than it does in Hughes's poem, but ultimately what Davie is dreaming of – a language in which 'we should say . . . Not what we mean, but what / The words would mean', in which 'We should speak, / As carpenters work, / With the grain of our words' – is not so different from the *effect* Hughes sometimes achieves (when we fall under the spell of the gnat's crazy lexicon, for instance). In his quest for words as pure as the hues of colour under the light of Saint Ives, Davie also recognizes man's 'ingrained habit' of elevating 'Into the light of ideas / The colourful trades', a regretful recognition which is also at the centre of Hughes's drama. Moreover, in terms of diction, I should think that a foreign ear – an American's for example – would find Hughes's language just as lucid as Davie's language is 'chaste'. (This is the word he uses when writing of late eighteenth-century plain talk.) One might say that Hughes is a deeper or a more complex poet: where Davie detects an ingrained *habit*, Hughes detects a depraved second nature, centered in the brain's activities. On the other hand, one might judge Hughes (and Davie seems tentatively to have done this, in *Thomas Hardy and British Poetry*, p. 102) to be a poet struggling with perceptions of truths larger than awareness itself.

*

In summary one might say that Ted Hughes represents the extreme fringe of contemporary anti-rationalist, mythopoeic poetry. The principal modern predecessor is no doubt D. H. Lawrence. Other practitioners include Charles Tomlinson, Peter Redgrove, the American Robert Bly and, to an extent, Seamus Heaney. That Hughes's genius is so singularly fixed by non-social and uncommon experience has no doubt meant that his presence has provoked mixed results from admiring younger poets. Since his path is set against anything remotely derivative (even verse forms), it has been healthy as a signal for those who know how to do their own thing. But as an influence or a model – as these exist in modern 'masters' like John Betjeman or Philip Larkin – Ted Hughes has probably forced more uncomfortable poses than he has encouraged young shamans to develop their personal magic. In this sense, Hughes's breed is always without direct issue, unlike that of poets of the 'Movement' who count already a number of solid and stylish followers, like Douglas Dunn and several 'Martian' poets. Hughes's real influence is very limited and very great at once, like Samuel Beckett's. As a force to bring about the individual idiom, his role is important, but as a model or master it is marginal, as much in the British Isles as in America or Australia.

3

LOOKING FOR A VOICE: 'THE HAWK IN THE RAIN', 'LUPERCAL', 'WODWO'

> Doth the hawk fly in thy wisdom, *and* stretch her wings toward the south?
> Doth the eagle mount up at thy command, and make her nest on high?
> She swelleth and abideth on the rock, upon the crag of the rock, and the strong place.
> From thence she seeketh her prey, *and* her eyes behold afar off.
> Her young ones also suck up blood: and where the slain *are* there *is* she. (Job 39: 26–30)

So far this book has been concerned with the main dramatic, psychological and interpretive problems in Hughes's work. In establishing the importance of these problems, I deliberately neglected questions of poetic development, of poetic form and of finding a voice for transmitting the extraordinary insights to which the poet has been made a party. All of these questions may be put as one: how and with what voice does one write poetry if one wishes to speak as if one *were*, in part, the amazing hawk and the daunting eagle mentioned in the book of Job? For the author of Job the role of the hawk and the eagle is to show us how puny we are and how great God is. This truth is spoken objectively; its rhetorical power derives from the series of deprecating questions – Could *you* make the hawk fly? Can *you* command the eagle?, etc. Internalizing a reality as colossal as this, finding poetic forms which complement the subjective perspective, all prove a considerable challenge for Hughes from his earliest poems in *The Hawk in the Rain* right up to the latest poems of *Wodwo*, roughly from 1955 to 1967. In the present chapter I wish therefore to look more closely at a group of problems which all perhaps stem from a general one, which is the problem of voice or of tone.

As we saw in the previous chapter many poems in *The Hawk in the Rain* are concerned with presenting the special knowledge conveyed by intimidating eyes ('The Jaguar', 'The Thought-Fox', 'Meeting', 'Wind', 'Childbirth', 'Law in the Country of Cats', 'The Casualty', 'Bayonet Charge' and 'The Martyrdom of Bishop Farrar'). As some titles indicate, the revelations are associated with a number of extraordinary moments of life – the delirium of childbirth, of death and dying. One senses a problem often in the relationship between lesser self and the superior or visionary self, because the poet appears to align himself more with the superior self than with the inferior self. Instead of a psychodrama, the imbalance between the two voices turns some poems into caricatures of the ordinary self. The vision then weighs heavily, like a badge of achievement, and the poetry begins to be argumentative and approaches rhetorical posturing.

In 'Egg-Head', for instance, Hughes's goal is to show how this lesser self works. The Egg-Head swells with pride for having reduced all of sensual life into a mild-mannered, vicarious 'Peeping through . . . fingers at the world's ends, / Or at an ant's head' (*HR*, p. 35). But if we think of the heroic figures of energy – the jaguar, the black goat of 'Meeting' (*HR*, p. 39) – we sense here more an ironic and even ridiculing comparison than a credible exploration of the Egg-Head's problems. The voice of the poet wants to isolate and heap scorn on this figure rather than bring him into the internal debate that elsewhere captivates us. The same effect is achieved in 'The Man Seeking Experience Enquires his Way of a Drop of Water' (*HR*, pp. 37–8), where the drop of water's contemptuous response nearly blasts this normal person to bits.

The sense of pride in achievement, the caricature of the lesser self, the unsettling juxtaposition – all are part of the problem of voice and tone which shows up in the prosody as well. This central problem manifests itself in a more general formal unevenness in the early verse. Hughes's sense of poetic form, up to the later poems of *Wodwo*, is sometimes perplexing and certainly unhelpful to the reader grappling with the 'meaning'. When he speaks later on of *real* man being visceral and audial rather than visual and conceptual, one understands why, until the late 1960s, metrical prosody is such an embarrassment for him, even at an intuitive level. Children's verse excepted, Hughes's poetry has a syllabic dimension only up to *Wodwo*, after which sense stress and the syntactic unit (comma, full stop, caesura, etc.) – all along trying to come to the fore – finally take over completely.

In 'Things Present' (*L*, p. 9), for example, there is a mixture of rhyming, half-rhyming and visual rhyming, syllabism and (as far as I can detect) purposeless running on, even between stanzas. 'My hands', we are told,

> Embody a now, erect a here
> A bare-backed tramp and a ditch without fire
>
> Cat or bread; . . .

Not only is this stunningly abstract, but metre, enjambement and even syntax are straining under what little the poet has to say. The evidence of these lines, and others at this period, shows that how the poet says things is, for the moment, quite separate in his mind from what he says. In 'Sunstroke' (*L*, p. 59) Hughes sets out with couplets, but, already in the second pair, the sentence has taken over effective control of the form, as can be heard in the enjambement 'Through a red heat / The cradled guns . . .' and later in the enjambement of the couplet-stanza (9 and 10):

> I lay healing
> Under the ragged length of a dog fox
>
> That dangled head downward from one of the beams,
> With eyes open, forepaws strained at a leap –
>
> Also surprised by the rain. (Couplets 9, 10 and 11)

The whole conceptual set of conventions is at odds with Hughes's effective sources of rhythm. This situation is not really resolved until the late poems of *Wodwo* where the whole notion of the metrical line gives way to semantic groups, the syntagm, or even the single word. These are the units that dominate *Crow* from beginning to end, where, as Hughes has said, he returned to a kind of 'natural' verse art which he had not used since he was a 19-year-old (Interview II, p. 212), to a prosody 'autochthonous and complete . . . with the minimum of cultural accretions' (*Art*, p. 107). In some respects the remarkable separateness of metre or mental prosodic forms, such as the syllabic line and the stanza, from the 'content', the semantic unit, is typical of Hughes's early prosody. One could also view the problem as being symptomatic of the poet's own moral quest, to put the spirit back into the body, the body back into the mind. Prosodically and morally, the two sides of man are not so much reconciled in the early works as demonstrated and objectified through strongly weighted comparisons in favour of visceral, energetic man. Just as we may feel the thinking self, the visual/conceptual man, is not being healed as much as he is being pointed at and put to shame, so, in prosodic terms, we are struck by a certain amount of superfluous metrical and stanzaic formalism the poet does not as yet know how to integrate into the 'body' of his verse.

There are a number of fine poems in *Lupercal*, none the less: 'Hawk Roosting' and 'Pike' (*L*, pp. 26, 56–7), already discussed, are for good reason favourite choices for school and university anthologies. Of the former, in which we have an extraordinary humanized anti-human brain thinking, Hughes has made the following comments which can be read as having a general relevance to the whole of *Lupercal* and to the problem of interiorizing the superior knowledge of the voice which speaks in Job:

> what I had in mind was that in this hawk Nature is thinking. Simply Nature. It's not so simple maybe because Nature is no longer simple. I intended some Creator like the Jehovah of Job but more feminine. When Christianity kicked the devil out of Job what they actually kicked out was Nature . . . and Nature became the devil. He doesn't sound like Isis, mother of the gods, which he is. He sounds like Hitler's familiar spirit. There is a line in the poem almost verbatim from Job. (Interview I, p. 8)

This is an explanation of a further glimpse of that double world of the hawk's eye: 'Nature thinking' sums it all up, both from the poet's perspective and from the reader's. And so do the sexual questions Hughes raises with regard to the bird whose 'manners are tearing off heads'. Just as human nature (perhaps what Edmund Burke called second nature – here, also Christianity) has split matter and mind, so an original being of an androgynous or bi-sexual nature must have also been lost or split rigidly into female-body and male-brain. This is why the hawk, mother Nature, seems to us so 'masculine' and blood-thirsty. In reality it is *we* who have suppressed body, have turned it into the slightly monstrous being that the dreaming hawk reveals herself to be. (This is the same suppression responsible in the story 'Sunday' for creating the stark polarity between an effeminate dreamer Michael and an animalistic rat man, Billy Red.) Hughes says that 'Nature is no longer simple' but the point about a human trying to imagine *natural* thought is that perceived brutality is inseparable from, indeed eloquent commentary upon, the psychology of the perceiver – the poet himself, that is, who feels the need to write a poem, and the reader, who seeks in vain to a find a position in relation to it. Ultimately, of course, the reader needs to identify not only with the opposing forces the poet sends off to battle but also with the healing process which this battle is supposed to assist. The problem of the early poems, for the reader at least, is that the battle often seems to be 'out there', objectified, as though Hughes were writing with the same voice as the author of Job. Thus our relation to the mythic or healing process, and to the poet who instigates this process, is difficult to perceive.

Just as metre in the making of his lines seems to be at odds with, or not yet complementary to, Hughes's moral quest, so the self-distancing which objective narration requires (though this distance may often prove to be more apparent than real) is relatively rare and comparatively unsuccessful in the early verse. When, in his poetry, Hughes treats myth objectively (like the author of Job), in telling or re-telling stories, he writes with a borrowed pen, in a mode that does not really suit. In the title poem of the volume *Lupercal*, 'Lupercalia', Hughes makes use of an actual Roman rite in a fashion which, compared to the more subjective myth-making or fishing 'For what might move, for what eye might move' ('Pike', *L*, p. 57), appears distant and clumsy. The ancient sequence of events in the fertility ritual, which the poem recounts, has the effect of impeding the subjective quest for renewal because the narrator has to get the 'facts' of the story right. Alternating between the personal quest and the duty of narrating proves to be a real embarrassment which makes the ritual sound like a bit of bizarre folklore, as alien personally to the subjective voice one senses in the poem as from the poem's uninitiated, twentieth-century readers. No single short passage could demonstrate how inert the old Roman ritual remains in this fifty-line poem, but the important general point here is the degree to which Hughes's art seems ill at ease when using any ready-made material, either a ready-to-use metrical form or a hand-me-down legend. This orientation has notable consequences (especially for us readers) when one recalls that most of our society's myths operate under conditions of a high degree of objectivity, as in the myths or hypotheses upon which our scientific explanations repose (e.g. of causality, substance or capacity). The same problem of 'Lupercalia' comes across in other poems with an objective side, such as 'The Perfect Forms' (*L*, p. 51), 'Logos', 'Theology', 'Karma' or 'Wings' (*W*, pp. 34, 149, 160–1, 174–6) or, to a lesser degree, in 'Crow's Account of St George' (*C*, pp. 31–2). For example, in 'The Perfect Forms' Hughes writes about real, historical people: Socrates, 'complacent as a phallus', or Buddha, 'whose one thought fills immensity'. These founders of formal religions are then compared to the poem's hero,

> This monstrous-headed difficult child!
> Of such is the kingdom of heaven.

It seems as if the personal or questing voice has completely disappeared. And the reader finds himself in the unpleasant position of trying to decide whether to read the poem objectively – as a statement about the fundamental buffoonery of the founders of the world's great religions (when compared to the child) – or to grope for another perspective, which, in this poem, is virtually unavailable. This unsure footing becomes like quick-sand, when we try to understand why Hughes has taken a line out of Blake ('Prisons are built with stones of Law, Brothels with bricks of Religion . . . The cistern contains: the fountain overflows. One thought fills immensity.' – *The Marriage of Heaven and Hell*, 'Proverbs of Hell', plate 8). Is Blake used to prop up the argument or to give it another, cultural dimension?

Hence, when we think of Hughes's most successful early poems and the subjective point of view from which they are written, poetry that moves in the direction of 'Lupercalia' or 'The Perfect Forms' is always about to open a Pandora's box of misguided (though implicitly justified) reactions: Has he got the story right? Where does the story come from? What did it mean for the

Romans? What kind of religion did Socrates found? Did not the Buddha teach *submission* to Nature, etc.

Being the tailpiece of *Lupercal*, 'Lupercalia' attempts to bring the whole collection into the focus of the spring ritual, so resolving the tension that dominates the larger part of the book. Hughes makes this sort of gesture an explicit part of his strategy in *Wodwo* (1967):

> The stories and the play in this book may be read as notes, appendix and unversified episodes of the events behind the poems, or as chapters of a single adventure to which the poems are commentary and amplification. Either way, the verse and the prose are intended to be read together, as parts of a single work. (W, p. 9)

This sounds like desperate pleading, but this note by the author is fully consonant with the subjective quest in which the writing of each and every piece has participated. Indeed, adding together all the parts of *Wodwo* yields, objectively, nothing of much outward coherence – no recurring characters, no refrains and no single 'plot'. The stories were mostly written around 1960, the poems between 1960 and 1966. During this period Hughes mentally followed his former wife through the lych gate, in poems like 'Ghost Crabs', 'Song of a Rat' and 'The Howling of Wolves', the darkest, perhaps, he has ever written. Then, for nearly three years, he wrote very little poetry, until in 1966 a trip to Ireland brought forth 'Skylarks' and 'Gnat-Psalm', little masterpieces of movement and light.

Wodwo is the first collection to have the degree of sub-textual integument, the sort of intellectual and emotional unity, that distinguishes a sequence from an anthology and which gives each individual poem an extra resonance. As an inner quest, *Wodwo* is the mental process of disencumberment that leads to wodwo-hood, life as a wild man, amongst wolves and serpents, bulls and bears, wild boars and giants in the rocky fells past which rides the slayer of the dragon Nature (according to Hughes). (The quotation in which the wodwo is mentioned comes from the late fourteenth-century poem *Sir Gawain and the Green Knight*, ll. 720–4, which mention the arrogant knight's battle with the wild man.) True knighthood, true obeisance to Nature, Hughes implies, lies in the rudimentary being within us, possessed primarily of the older of the two nervous systems, which mind should serve through mythic activity alone. The wodwo wants all the world to be a part of him, and – amazingly or miraculously – he *does not know why*:

> why do I find
> this frog so interesting as I inspect its most secret
> interior and make it my own? (*W*, p. 183)

This individual is a much more credible exteriorization of a subjective search than the fawning spectacle of 'Lupercalia' or the voice-from-on-high in 'The Perfect Forms' or 'Theology'. One can feel in 'Wodwo' a narrator attempting to submit himself, through a series of childlike questions, to wodwo-hood, to what is neither a thing nor a person, but a state of mind. The wodwo is a state of being that does not yet provoke the ghastly stare of Nature's eye; in a word the wodwo is virtually an unbordered 'I' that expands in the marshes, on the fells, inside a frog, up and down weeds, trees and roots.

Moving down to a wodwo standard of living is treated pedagogically, so to speak, in 'Skylarks' and 'Gnat-Psalm' (*W*, pp. 168–71, 179–81), poems already commented upon in the first chapter. With reference to 'Wodwo', one should add here that if the wodwo spoke a language it might be like the 'natural' *Ursprache* that the gnats teach to the poet, taking with their dancing swarms, their crazy 'lexicons', his own staring skull. The relationship of man, the subject, and Nature, the object, is here abolished, and the staring poet is more like the marionette celebrated in Kleist's famous dialogue, *On the Puppet Theatre*, which is set in motion by the dancing fingers of a divine puppeteer. It is also important here that the narrator is being conducted to wodwo-hood through his eyes. The gnats conquer the 'staring skull' because they have cast a charm against visual/conceptual man and the organ which Hughes believes to be intimately connected to *Homo sapiens*'s waywardness. Thanks to the gnat's dance-language, the eye is filled with movement and invisibility rather than stability and objects.

At this point in his development as a poet (one might speak more accurately of a chastening regression), Hughes's prosody marches in step with his meaning. From 1966 or so onwards, with few exceptions, the poet's lines are strung out to reflect and comment on, visually and sonorously, the elements of meaning. Here is a short excerpt from 'Skylarks' which describes the upward flight of the bird:

> A whippet head, barbed like a hunting arrow,
>
> But leaden
> With muscle
> For the struggle
> Against
> Earth's centre.
>
> And leaden
> For ballast
> In the rocketing storms of the breath.
>
> Leaden
> Like a bullet
> To supplant
> Life from its centre. (W, p. 168)

The effect is something like the last stanza of Verlaine's delightful 'Chanson d'automne', where rhythmically and visually a falling leaf swoops and turns, falls and slides, twirls and sways to the ground, exteriorizing the autumnal feeling within:

> Et je m'en vais
> Au vent mauvais
>   Qui m'emporte
> Deçà, delà
> Pareil à la
>   Feuille morte.

In 'Skylarks' the rhythmic effect of imitating the bird's struggle against gravity, the transformation of lead into muscle and then into ballast, i.e. rising higher and higher, is based on the little rises and falls of the syntagm or the single word. There being a short or long pause after line and stanza endings (this is how Hughes himself interprets them in reading this sort of poem), when we read 'In the rocketing storms of the breath' or other long lines, we

61

have a real feel of coasting or diving or uninterrupted flight. This long line moreover seems to give the bird a few seconds to renew its energies and shoot off, hell for leather, as it gulps for air. There is, I feel, a slight and pleasurable shock at the running-on of 'supplant / Life from its centre', as though, after two lines of falling sounds, one were pulled sonorously into the extraordinary notion and difficult visual image of life being supplanted from its centre. Where Verlaine uses sounds and an explicit simile to tell us of his inner feelings, Hughes is much more circumspect, much more private. But, ultimately, he is training his imagination and the rhythms of his own breathing to imitate, if for only a second, the 'conscience perfect' of the lark.

The quest of *Wodwo* begins with 'Thistles' (*W*, p. 17), a poem about the hostility that man senses in the natural cycles – 'Everyone a revengeful burst / Of resurrection' – and with 'Still Life' (*W*, p. 18) that compares a moorland, which expects 'to be in at the finish' of the world, and the ephemeral harebell, which 'Any known name of blue would bruise'. The stillness of the poet's moorland picture only becomes clear when one realizes that the apparent personifications of the rock, said to have *fingers*, of the flower, said to have *veins*, and of the sea, whose *womb* will engulf both of them one day, are just inert concepts or stillnesses in his mind which separate him from the landscape he tries in vain to appropriate with words. The reader here is brought up with a shock to recognize in this personification the voice of the silent narrator (the poet behind his poem), prodding painfully his inert self with his active, mobile self. The voice we hear is one which cannot account for or live within the most extreme forms of the one cycle which begins with the sea and will end with the sea. The stillness inside is what makes this voice resist the adequacy of Nature as a mirror for the forming intelligence. This is where the quest of *Wodwo* ends, with submission to gnat-language and the indiscriminate perspective of the wodwo, both reflections of Nature's ever-moving, un-still-life mirror.

4

THE BODY AS PRISONER: 'SENECA'S OEDIPUS', 'ORGHAST', 'CROW', 'CAVE BIRDS'

What Crow is grappling with is not 'something dangerous' but what becomes at the end of all his mistakes and errantry – his bride and almost his humanity. To every action, an equal but opposite reaction: in their alarming aspect, the transformation images are mirror-images of his method of interrogation. The hidden thing defends itself with these. (*Study*, p. 257 – letter of October 1979)

If, in the beginning, there is that extraordinary, part-human organ, the eye – of the sheer cliff, of the hawk, of the jaguar, of the black goat, of the pike – with its power not just to frighten but to insinuate itself into the most deeply felt desires and urges, then, just after the beginning, there is revenge. Yet, revenge makes the eye only more evil and more fascinating, because in revenge is attacked, instinctively, what first was felt as desire (i.e. what first declared itself to belong to what is least aware in man, instinct itself). This wound which worsens with attention represents the basic psychological condition of the drama with which Hughes's 'middle' work – from the late 1960s to the early or mid-1970s – is concerned.

I noted above how Hughes's analysis of a sheer cliff led, as if automatically, to an image of mountaineers whose main reason for climbing was to gratify an urge to hit back at the intimidating heights. In the following quotations, written five years later in 1968, there is a similar analysis of the 'evil eye' with particular reference to science, puritanism and myth. The use of the word *prestige*, an attitudinal cognate of fascination, is particularly interesting, because we see that, in reality, Christianity does not so much kick Nature out of religion as shore up its powers by retaining a perverse *hold* on Nature right where it matters most: in one's body, in one's instincts:

> The scientific attitude, which is the crystallization of the rational attitude, has to be passive in face of the facts if it is to record the facts accurately. The scientist has to be a mirror first. He has to be a mirror second too, because the slightest imaginative bias in his presentation of the facts invalidates his findings and reflects badly on his standing as a scientist. And such is the prestige of the scientific style of mind that this passivity in the face of the facts, this detached, inwardly inert objectivity, has become the prevailing mental attitude of our time. It is taught in schools as an ideal. The result is something resembling mental paralysis (Myth I, p. 56). A scientifically biased education has produced a chronically sick society. . . . we have now just such a state of apathy – detached, impersonal passivity – towards our inner life, as we have towards the mountainous outer world of facts and actions (Myth I, p. 60). It's no accident that puritanism, and the puritanical outlook, runs absolutely parallel to the materialist, scientific outlook, because both oppose the whole world of nature. . . . In other words [our culture's archetypal stories, like St George destroying evil] put us into a world that doesn't really exist, except within a very narrowly puritan society (Myth I, p. 69).

These quotations all derive from the same lecture, quoted above, apropos *The Iron Man*. Hughes is clearly drawing as much on his own education and the attitudes it encouraged as on poetic theory à la Robert Graves. A few years after the thoughts above, Hughes edited a collection of Shakespeare's poetry. Here is part of what he says, in the afterword to that anthology, about our culture's favourite stories, in particular those which attracted Shakespeare:

> The Shakespearean fable, in other words, is really the account of how, in the religious struggle that lasted from the middle of the sixteenth century to the middle of the seventeenth, England lost her soul. To call this event a 'dissociation of sensibility' is an understatement. Our national poems are tragedies for a good reason. (*Shakespeare*, p. 197)

Leaving aside whether this interpretation of the 'dissociation of sensibility' is justified or not, one can see here, in the pattern of all Hughes's reasoning on matters religious, educational and archetypal, a recurrent attitude that is associated in the poetry with the normal self. This normal self, which finds the hawk menacing and so lies outside real God or Nature, is none the less part of an extraordinary self that knows about the rightness of the hawk or the God it witnesses. The normal self is linked with a scientific objectivity that moves hand-in-glove with Puritanism and its world of facts. But the silent narrator (the voice the reader may feel as the poet himself or the strange presence of a listener or witness), who is in touch with both ordinary and extraordinary selves, knows that facts are not just facts; he knows that they are part of an unnerving and elaborate *fiction*, which passes for irrefragable truth and thus conveys prestige, in the sense in which Hughes uses the word: that which overpowers the mind and incites passivity. A second and even more pertinent meaning of the word is also implied, that of legerdemain, prestidigitation, magic, curse – in a word, the force that makes 'facts' a primitive and immovable fiction.

Where the fiction comes from is hard to say, and to try, as I have done, to relate it to Mount Zion Christianity is only one stab in a general direction which, in the quotation above, we see extended into English history, literature, science, education and the rest. However, what should be kept clear is the mechanism of the inner drama that such a 'prestige' fiction sets in motion. Revenge is the general rubric for this, but the roles of the revengers, the wounded and the avenged – extraordinary self, ordinary self, and silent narrator – are as rich psychologically as they can be at times confusing.

Several consequences follow from the observation about prestige-fictions and revenge. First, what the normal self sees is as much an extraordinary glimpse of another, natural reality as it is an imperious fiction *of its own self* (as made aware by the self that reveals this glimpse). Second, the narrator or Hughes, the poet, is less a person made privy to the extraordinary glimpses of truth than a person with a double albatross around his neck, both of revelation and of an awareness of the prestige of some loathsome fiction or body of 'facts'. His role, therefore, develops not just as a fiction maker – a poet turning sensory experience into verse – but as an exorcist who must first of all unravel the complicated evil spell of a deeply rooted fiction, like the one that makes mountaineers seek 'revenge' against the mountain. The point is that the mountaineer's revenge, like the poet's, is no exorcism. If anything, it makes the spell cast by the mountain even more powerful. Thus Hughes's fiction almost always involves a tragedy before revenge and the quest for truth, purloined by the primitive evil spell, can begin. In the familiar context of Genesis 3:7 one could say that the initial tragedy of Hughes's work is an exorcist's first response to an evil spell of aprons:

> And the eyes of them both were opened, and they knew they *were* naked; and they sewed fig leaves together, and made themselves aprons.

And the complexity of the response is owing to the fact that the spell is cast by censorious eyes which have themselves taken the body prisoner.

*

In his first interview with Egbert Faas, Hughes said that every writer develops either outwardly, towards history and society, or inwardly, organizing his mental world and searching there the patterns of his mythology (Interview I, pp. 14–15). With the exception of *The Iron Man*, whose audience largely determined the outward-looking mode of the story, I think the sense of Hughes's development is clear. The internalization of the eye's special glimpse points at the real drama that concerns him.

This inner drama is addressed primarily as a release of the body from an overwhelming or prestigious fiction and, following this, a re-organ-ization, in which the image of the extraordinary vision of the ideal Eye is paramount (the play on ideality and sensuality is intentional). This inner direction may well have been urged on Hughes by Peter Brook's request that he prepare a new version of Seneca's *Oedipus* for The National Theatre Company in 1967. Certainly, contact with this modern proponent of Artaud's Theatre of Cruelty was as important as the Oedipus theme itself. The ruling images of Antonin Artaud's theory of the renewed body come from his essay on the bubonic plague, the peculiar

66

feature of which is to kill the subject whilst leaving his organs intact. Theatre, says Artaud, should have a similar aim: to create a new organ-ism with the old organs.

After *Wodwo*, Hughes wrote three works that do move inward, toward the prisoner, the body, in the spirit of Artaud's theory. The works are the adaptation of Seneca's *Oedipus*, which was played in 1968 and first published in 1969; the sequence of poems, *Crow, From the Life and Songs of Crow* (1970), and, most radically, the project for a play called *Orghast*, which sadly remains extant only as notes, remarks, reports and drawings in A. C. H. Smith's account, *Orghast at Persepolis* (1972), and in other articles and interviews. All three works show the extent to which the 'space-bat-angel-dragon' *out there*, in *The Iron Man*, is rooted familiarly and insidiously as a stoney sphinx *within*.

In Hughes's reworking of *Oedipus*, the role of the frightening eye is played by the sphinx. Jocasta, here, becomes random sexuality, body deprived of spirit, while Oedipus is lined up with the corrupt brain god, who hoards spirit, keeping it out of body at all costs. This results in the plague of Thebes, which is just another aspect of aimless physical mutation allied to Jocasta's wantonness. The sphinx forms a psychological focus in the play and is important as a precursor of other sphinx-like taboos that will be central to the drama of *Crow* and *Orghast*: 'her face was a gulf[,] her gaze paralysed her victims' (*O*, p. 18). In fact, Oedipus' first monologue (*O*, pp. 13–16), which follows the chorus's description of the plagued city, is really a dialogue between him and an internalized sphinx. His method of working off a curse by trying to counter-charm it recurs time and again in *Crow*. Just as Oedipus thinks aloud about the sphinx, so a silent narrator in nearly every poem of *Crow* sends out a sort of psychological advocate to try to loosen the sensual hold of the brain-teasing female body, i.e. censured desire. The goal of both works points toward releasing or remaking the old body and focuses this effort upon the essential parts – the organs and especially the eye. Oedipus fails to renew his organs, for tearing out his eyes leaves him more desensualized than blind – in the special sense in which blindness may be attributed to the perfect organ of sight, the sun, whose blind gaze animates all: 'blacker / Than any ... negro's eye-pupil. / ... like the sun, / Blacker / Than any blindness'

(C, p. 66). The ideal body or organ which the silent narrator wants to release from the sphinx's charming custody would thus be, like the sun, an exclusively transitive active organ, taking in nothing and suffusing all with its own streaming motion.

Though Thebes is ultimately freed of the curse of the plague when, blind, Oedipus quits his kingdom, Oedipus himself still belongs to the sphinx. A slave describes Oedipus' near literal re-organ-ization: 'his hands kept griping at his stomach / he was trying to tear himself open / to gouge out the bowels and liver and heart[,] the whole mass of agony' (O, p. 49); this ends with 'rags of flesh strings and nerve ends still trailing over his cheeks' (O, p. 51). Oedipus, following Seneca, appears here simply to be paying his respects to the horror of fate. Yet, in Hughes's handling, one feels that his actions constitute a radical attempt to kill part of his body that an imperious fiction (i.e. the sphinx) has taken captive ('her gaze paralysed her victim'). Even Oedipus seems to realize that demystifying the sphinx (unravelling her fiction) is not simple self-mutilation. This, he seems to know, is exactly where the US Army, in the Invader-from-Outer-Space movie, goes wrong, when it pulverizes the monstrous intruder. To destroy the alien body, the prisoner of the sphinx, is no way to exorcize her riddle:

> the light   that awful eye   that never let me rest and
> followed me everywhere   peering through every crack
>   at last you've escaped it   you haven't driven it
> away   you haven't killed that as   you killed your father
>   it's abandoned you   left you to yourself   sim-
> ply   it's left you to your new face   the true face of
> Oedipus (O, p. 53)

Having separated his mother and father, Jocasta and Laius, Oedipus goes on to commit the ultimate crime, which is to refuse, either as son or as husband, the body of Jocasta: in this way, he *confirms* the corruptness of her body and participates indirectly in keeping spirit out of the body (in Hughes's version, Jocasta sinks the sword of patricide into her *neck*, thus underscoring the image of total dissociation of mind and body). It is clear that Oedipus' new vision, his blindness, in no way imitates that of the sun described in 'Crowcolour', quoted above. Seneca's play is really about driving out the monster from the community (the chorus celebrates this deliverance: 'lift your faces   now you will see the skies alter   and the sun and the grass   everything will change', O, p. 55). Hughes's play, on the other hand, is above all about the sphinx and the pathos of submitting to her gaze in the act of self-mutilation, the act thought most likely to unfasten and destroy her empire. Blind Oedipus leaves Thebes to wander for ever, still spiritually dominated by the gaze.

Working with another man's material, Hughes must have felt Oedipus to be an intriguing discovery, in so far as he could serve as advocate, scapegoat and sacrificial victim for the sphinxes lurking in the eyes which had always unnerved him. If one thinks of Crow as an Oedipus some silent narrator uses as just such a surrogate, one unlocks one of the key problems of perspective in this revolutionary book of poems.

The first 'Crow' poems were written in late 1966 or early 1967, while Hughes was working on Oedipus, and the last as late as 1975. The first British edition of Crow, From the Life and Songs of Crow (1970) was augmented by new poems in the first American edition of 1971, then by one more poem in the second English edition of 1972, which has remained unchanged. In June 1971, when the majority of 'Crow' poems had been written, Hughes was once again called upon by Peter Brook to write a new play for production in Iran. It is useful to look first at this remarkable experiment, which also focuses on the role of Oedipus, because – though it is later than most of Crow – it objectifies with great lucidity this book's complex subjective drama.

Orghast draws on the ancient story of Prometheus, on Calderón's La Vida es Sueño (also of Iranian origin), on Blake, and on tales derived from Manichean tradition. Yet the play is more than a collation of these sources; it is pre-eminently an attempt to work out objectively a whole cosmology. Moreover – most impressive and most difficult – it is a search for primeval sounds that precede the sonorous and symbolic stability that is necessary for language as communication. Following the spirit of Artaud and Brook, Hughes attempts to discover or create a form of body language in which sounds themselves *mean* – rather than stand as symbolic counters for something else. Again, it emphasizes audial/visceral man over visual/cerebral man, though Hughes's search, in so far as it seeks an unmediated system of sensual signs, is comparable to Ernest Fenollosa's work on the Chinese ideogram and the movement into non-symbolic calligraphy in the work of painters like Michaud, Hartung, Mathieu and Riopelle. The significance of this new kind of language is highlighted by the fact that the whole of *Orghast* is meant to take place *within the body* of Prometheus on his rock (*Orghast*, p. 91); so the narrative is really part of human physiology, not human symbology. Here, in quotations from *Orghast* and *Oedipus*, we see how Hughes aims to chant away the old body – or, linguistically, the sensuous sound that is attached to superfluous conceptual meaning – to clear the mental system for acceptance of virtually pure sounds, more potent and direct than old word-sounds:

        OOO-AI-EE . . . KA
        CHANT   3 times
        REPLY   3 times

        DANCE DEATH INTO ITS HOLE
        DANCE DEATH INTO ITS HOLE
        INTO ITS HOLE
        ITS HOLE

        ITS HOLE . . . (*O*, p. 30)

        OOOL NEEEE-YAGH
        OOOL O NEEEAAR   NEEY-AGH
        OOOOOL O BOH
        BYOOOOSHD
        BIKK OGH
        NEEEY AGH   AGHAAAR . . . (*Orghast*, pp. 116–17)

The latter passage is translated as meaning 'Woman has opened / woman has opened life / woman your death / secret thing / your replacement / has opened future has opened . . .' The strategy is to win back the ear from its sensuous sublimation in words – just as Hughes's future Oedipus advocates will strive to retrieve body or instinct held captive by the sphinx. Behind the power of the chant which Hughes invokes lies the intuition that the power of the sphinx, the taboo, is proportionally related to the desire that it sublimates. To repossess this desire in all its purity, it is necessary to call up the near hypnotic power of pure sound, of words emptied of conceptual content (which is itself inseparable from the primal, prestigious fiction which the sphinx deploys as 'facts', or, in the story, as the riddle): this represents the first stage of demystifying the evil eye.

The story of *Orghast* seeks to accomplish a similar exorcism as the audience allows itself to 'identify', to merge emotionally, with Prometheus' coming to terms with his taboo – the vulture (yet another hawk's eye). Life being (ORG) and flame-spirit (GHAST) constitute the meaning of the title's sound; the narrative concerns their separation, by visual/conceptual man, and the attempts to reunite them in the persons of a number of precursors of Prometheus, all of whom are now part of his body on the rock (as fettered instinct, feeling and memory). The central demon and sphinx of the drama is KROGON, son of the perfect harmony of spirit and body – the sun's light permeating the earth's surface, intellectual man fully suffused in woman's body. But Krogon lives in time (natural cycles conceptualized). The awareness of insecurity in 'changing' time provokes in the first place his desire to cling, to resist change, and thus separate mind (unmoving) and matter (ever recurring). An era of meaningless reproduction and purposeless suffering (the siblings of the same dissociation) follows. Krogon sires a succession of children who try in vain to overthrow him. Their unsuccessful revenge against his spiritual repression only makes him more anxious to control the lives of his offspring. These children are partly a product of MOA – earth body, the original wife of SUN (spirit), now a wanton, Jocasta-like mindless body – and Krogon, whose bodily functions, though reduced to the basics of sex, still bring forth new generations. Moa continues to produce Krogon's children, with the sole hope that one of them will depose the mad brain god and reunite her with Sun. Yet, with every revenge, Krogon becomes craftier and more mechanical, consolidating his monstrous hold on pre-revenge instincts by turning them into elements of an unquestionable fiction. His own, early instinctual life is just as dangerous to his rising ego as are his sons. His dominion rests upon his building up an impenetrable taboo system so as to neutralize both his heirs and his own body-self or waning *alter ego*.

One challenger of note, ALGOLUZ – a version of Herakles, hero of physical deeds – fails where his intellectual counterpart

SOGIS finally wins. The mental revenger is the only one able to cast a counter-riddle capable of lifting the censure that is vital to Krogon's taboo. Once this occurs, Sogis marries USSA who had first inspired him when a prisoner by giving him all the trapped light of Krogon's previous victims. Now married to true body and endowed with the ancient spirit that escaped (as dead matter) the father's desperate control, Sogis disassembles Krogon's defences and charms him into submission. This finally restores the unity of matter spiritualized and spirit materialized, as it may be imagined when the sun shone upon the earth, before the advent of man.

Since the whole play takes place inside the body of Prometheus or Pramanath, his Persian name, it is for him a uniquely subjective affair in both intellectual and corporal senses. Prometheus is, like man, at once eternal consciousness, capable of knowing eternity through the imagination, and body living in time and suffering. The two parts of man constitute the eternal dilemma of the rock to which Prometheus is chained. As one aspect of Krogon, the vulture is Nature eternally feeding upon man (i.e. both Nature being objectively eternal and awful and Nature being perceived as an eternal, demonic 'fact' of life). The idea of acting out Prometheus' whole story in his body reflects an attempt to forge what for both mind and senses is a purely corporal relationship with the dilemma. Only in this way can the insinuating fiction be, like Krogon, deposed, and a new body be set free.

This complicated story, itself but a fragment of much more detailed accounts given by Hughes to A. C. H. Smith and others, is immediately comprehensible if the narrative is subordinated to the poet's subjective motivation, which is to unravel and ultimately control the sinister psychology of the Krogon within one's self. *Crow*, in its totality, is just such an attempt to loosen the grip of the evil eye (alias the vulture, the sphinx, Krogon *et al.*). The difference that exists between looking at Hughes's work subjectively and objectively can be seen in the crossed wires of the following interview. Here Egbert Faas is asking about motifs, themes and so on; Hughes, thinking back on *Crow* much in the way he must have thought while writing it, gives more or less uncomprehending (though sincere) answers:

FAAS. One of the unifying devices in *Crow* . . . is the recurrence of particular themes. Especially complex is your symbolic use of notions of Laughter, Smiling and Grinning. . . . [Do] these notions stand for an acceptance of suffering and evil . . . ?

HUGHES. I'm not sure what they signify.

FAAS. Another recurrent motif is Crow eating in the face of adversity, in the face of suffering, violence etc. . . .

HUGHES. Most of them appeared as I wrote them. They were usually something of a shock to write. Mostly they wrote themselves quite rapidly, the story was a sort of machine that assembled them, and several of them that seem ordinary enough now *arrived with a sense of having done something . . . tabu*. It's easy enough to give interpretations I think and draw possibilities out of them but whether they'd be the real explanations I don't know. (Interview I, p. 18; my italics)

It is worth adding to this a short passage that follows the quotation from the letter Hughes wrote to Gifford and Roberts, cited at the beginning of the chapter:

The 'violence' of the poem, therefore, is limited to a purely psychological and even barely conscious event. It inheres in Crow's attitude to the hidden thing. (*Study*, p. 256 – letter of October 1979)

Readers have variously been struck by the 'violence' of *Crow*, its lack of overall unity, its comic-cartoon disjointedness and the sort of recurring 'themes' Faas mentions. Yet all these ways of looking at *Crow*, I feel, address the poems in the book as if they might have an important meaning on their own, separated from the moral purpose their writing has served, i.e. separated from some silent narrator's perspective. But the two personas one can often perceive in the poems are not only the result of a moral crisis but also the active agents of resolving the moral crisis. Indeed it is this sense of a fragmentation of voices which challenges our first 'aesthetic' reactions to the poems as objects or as objective narrations. But, as Hughes suggests himself in the first quotation, the poet used Crow as his advocate to unlock or confront the captive powers of some very personal, half-conscious taboo. Unlocking the taboo, as he says in the letter, is a way of turning a monster, Krogon, into a source of strength – a way, in fact, of recovering one's own fettered instincts.

Seen in a broader context, Crow's advocacy is comparable to

the literary and folkloric role played by many cultural heroes such as Merlin, Taliesin, Romulus or the magicians of Eleusis. Their main function is to explain, relate and join an emerging human form to the animal forms from which it springs. The context of *Crow* may be clarified by this anthropological definition of the generic character known as the 'trickster'. In reading or in listening to some ancient story told around the camp fire, we identify with the hero's provocations. We use him mentally to confront our own taboos or to help us to understand our relationship to the rest of the created world. Note as well that the cultural hero is not only a magician but is, like Crow, also distinguished by his incompetence or perverseness.

> [The trickster is a] character in world folklore who plays tricks on his adversaries or opponents. In North American Indian lore, he is usually the tribe's cultural hero . . . and is a combination of human and animal. Coyote is the best known North American Indian trickster. Often the trickster is on the side of the irrational and evil, but his victims are not pitied. He usually has an animal companion, which may be a foil for his cleverness or even cleverer than he. The trickster usually displays negative qualities, like stupidity and pretentiousness, or perhaps duplicity and other anti-social qualities, which may enable him to vanquish his opponents. Stories of the trickster are usually told to amuse an audience, which usually identifies with the trickster and thus symbolically asserts itself over the forces of the world and nature. The trickster may be killed, but it is understood that he can come back to life. (*Dictionary*, p. 547)

Interpreting exactly what 'the forces of the world and nature' represent, for us, for the Indian and for Ted Hughes is clearly important for understanding the specific character and function of the trickster. For Hughes's Crow, however, what is subdued is related to unreal forces; but this subduing is part of a larger submission to true Nature.

From this point of view, it may seem curious that the word that comes first to many of Hughes's British critics is 'violence'. This probably is just a reaction to the objective side of the poetry, to the so-called themes, motifs and devices which one notes when one is not alive to the need that brings them into being. What Hughes confronts are forces essentially like the monsters from outer space in the movies or the angel-dragon that the Iron Man battles with – except that they are, like Krogon, as strong as primitive urges are strong, and return, if denied, with even more power. This is why the answer lies with Sogis, the spiritual hero, not with Algoluz or Herakles, the physical hero: the body is hostage to a fiction and only a hero of anti-fiction, like Sogis, can free it. In the process, as Hughes says, a deep level of consciousness feels some sort of psychological violence, because a convention has already fictionalized this level of consciousness, as different kinds of reflexes and various humanized instincts.

Therefore, in *Crow*, the absence of a meaningful objective world (which we might feel to be genuinely important in writers like Pope or Balzac or even Wordsworth) is directly related to the kind of mental state the bird tries to acquire for Hughes, the silent narrator, a mental state dominated by organs of crowcolour: black and blind but streaming radiance like the sun. Thus the many aspects of the sphinx, against which Crow is sent out to battle, may be summed up for the reader as the demon of living objectively. (Hughes's comments on the 'scientific attitude' shows what this means in practical terms.) In this sense, the endless motion of Sisyphus, the ever-recurring pain of cycles for eternity-conscious Prometheus, represent a sort of irreducible moral model for the mind.

In 'Existential Song', a 'Crow' poem published in the *London Magazine* of July/August 1970 (now collected in *Achievement*, p. 328), the crucial role of perspective or mental state forms the actual topic of the piece. Someone is 'running for his life', the poem says, thinking that this is just how life has to be. But, then, deciding he is 'nobody's fool', he stops running and suddenly finds himself in a vast desert, thinking he has had his own back on Fate and the Universe. However,

> It was too late for him to realize
> That this was the dogs tearing him to pieces
> That he was, in fact, nothing
> But a dummy on a racetrack
>
> And life was being lived only by the dogs.

A double irony says here that not only does the race, in itself, have no pre-critical meaning, but that the person who says to himself, 'I'm nobody's fool', *begins*, with the arrogance evident in such a thought, the process that turns the absurd, Sisyphean race into a victory of the object (the idea of being in a race) over life (the mental Sisyphus, eternally transitive and active).

Crow's enemy wants him to hop outside the track and stare at the race. This is what St George, for instance, has perfected. He is another version of Krogon, a brain god who has perfected a riddle as enthralling as the sphinx's: 'a track of numbers racing towards an answer . . . He melts cephalopods [salt water molluscs, but also a pun on walking brains] and sorts raw numbers / Out of their dregs' (*C*, p. 31). Being the sum of his parts, George embodies and communicates the unholy thought of being in an absurd race. A teleological totalitarian, he sees each answer and each whole automatically imputed to each question and each part. This absolutism means, of course, that George must murder his origins and his future (the poem, 'Crow's Account of St George' (*C*, pp. 31–2) ends with wife and children lying in their own blood). But George's real power derives from the fact that he is made of crow-material. A note on the record sleeve of *Crow Read by Ted Hughes* (Claddagh CCT 9–10) from 1973 says: 'Crow's whole quest aims to locate and release his own creator, God's nameless hidden prisoner, whom he encounters repeatedly but always in some unrecognizable form.' Though instigator of the rule of Logos, of the unlivable concept, George is, all the same, made of body and instincts, identical to the human animal's – and this is where, perversely, his strengths come from.

As the poet's advocate, Crow is distinguished, like the Iron Man, in being at the outset almost totally disarmed. In 'Two Legends', 'Lineage' and 'Examination at the Womb Door' (*C*, pp. 13–15), Crow's advocacy seems to consist virtually in being an anti-body or an anti-organ or, perhaps more accurately, a purely non-fictional body:

> . . . without eye
> Black the within tongue . . .
> . . . the huge stammer
> Of the cry that, swelling, could not
> Pronounce its sun. (*C*, p. 13)

If George is the insidious principle of the teleological *fait accompli*, akin to the man who jumps out of life to look on, then Crow represents an urge for a body that the arch demon Logos, the answer-in-every-question-George, *cannot conceive*. This is one way of escaping or even paralysing George and his confrère the voyeur. But the advocate does not always come out on top, which means that the poet's two selves – Crow or the advocate and the superior self who is held prisoner – are constantly falling out or are failing to merge.

In 'A Horrible Religious Error', for instance, Crow comes against a typical St George *jeu d'esprit*, 'The Sphynx of the final fact'. God's prisoner (in the words of the record sleeve) has been taught all the subtle casuistry of a Krogon finishing school, for he appears as an 'earth-bowel brown' serpent (C, p. 45), that is, a natural, even human-natural creation, only a slight variation on Nature's irreducible part, the atom. Even God writhes to see his prisoner so shifty, 'With its alibi self twisted around it'. To the ordinary man in Crow, this serpent must be as forbidding as the hawk's eye, with its 'deaf and mineral stare' which overpowers. To the unconscious animal in Crow, confronted with *natural* syllables of language 'like the rustling of the spheres', the snake that claims a totally natural pedigree, even when he talks, melts the neck muscles that support the human brain world, thus capturing man and woman's instinctual life: '"Your will is our peace"', they say. But Crow, whose instincts are partly aware of what is going on (this is why he is useful as an advocate), 'beats the hell out of' the snake and eats it. His horrible religious error lies, subjectively for Hughes, in the unsuccessful attempt to come to terms with the daunting animal God has trained in his intellectual zoo. Crow's job is not to eat this subtle monster, not to ingest its body fiction, but to free it. Yet even this failure is part of the larger advocacy and exorcism which disciplines the whole book.

Hughes spoke of *Crow* as being 'created by God's nightmare's attempt to improve on man' (Interview I, p. 18). Otherwise stated, Crow is a surge of revolt in fully created, fully finished man – a revolt that is, as a nightmare is, mainly body (unconsciousness) and partly brain (the awareness of the nightmare). As an apparently sub-normal creature, *vis-à-vis* finished man, Crow's trickster role is to undo fully formed man, to recover the power and body lost to this full formation.

How this normal or 'finished' man came into being is suggested by 'Snake Hymn' (*C*, p. 87), a poem which deals with much more besides: neurosis, Christianity and Christian love. Jesus figures here much as does the camouflaged snake in 'A Horrible Religious Error'. Crucifixion – the consecration or giving up of the body for a belief, the doctrine of love in the case of Christianity – is portrayed as the beginning or the reinforcing of the horrible sphinx: body gives itself up, is subsumed by a sovereign fiction. The power of Christianity, says the poet, derives from the fiction of Christian love which rests upon the following syllogism: I am born of body; the suffering of my body proves how much I cling to my truth; surely such suffering can only be for what is true.

In all these appeals to believe in Christ's legacy, the poem says, body is sublimated by non-body truth, by doctrine – such as the humanized New Testament concept of love. This is dramatized in the poem by producing Christ as (literally) the body of truth. In reality he has captured and emprisoned body, like his successor George or his predecessor Krogon. 'Snake Hymn', with its 'love that cannot die . . . [the] skin of agony / To hang, an empty husk' on the cross, is an extraordinary analysis of the poet's neurosis and the complex God of the prisoner.

All this points, I think, to the degree to which the mood of *Crow* grows out of and is focused by the narrative possibilities Hughes discovered in *Oedipus*: '[adapting *Oedipus*] turned out to be useful. Because it was a specific type and weight of feeling. . . . It simply concentrated me' (Interview II, p. 212). In one of the several Oedipus-Crow poems, 'Oedipus Crow' (*C*, p. 43), we see the same pointless dismemberment as that emphasized in the adaptation. In the poem, Crow is assaulted by death, mummies, disease and finally a gravestone which traps his foot (all this runs parallel to the random carnage and chaotic body which the sphinx's definitive riddle provokes). Crow bites off his foot to free his body – just as Oedipus thinks he can free himself of the sphinx's stare by pulling out his eyeballs. Oedipus' less than relieved valediction to Thebes intimated that his troubles were just beginning; in 'Oedipus Crow', things get worse once Crow has freed himself from pestilence – his watch, for example,

'Gallops away in a cloud of corpse dust', i.e. body, already random and pestilential, joins up with the fiction of chronology which falsifies the reality of cycles. The psychology revealed here is vicious: not only does Crow surrender body to sphinx-time, but he hobbles away 'cheered by the sound of his [sacrificed] foot' whose absence is compensated for by a dubious confidence in his watch, life in time, outside Nature.

'Song for a Phallus' (*C*, pp. 75–7) – originally composed as a satyr song for the end of Brook's production of *Oedipus* – goes as deep as any poem in *Crow* into the real horrors of the sphinx, at this sort of interior level a far cry from the 'space-bat-angel-dragon' outside. The poem reveals the terrors of recognizing oneself suddenly to be out of the race, a voyeur, an object stared at by one's own eye:

> He split his Mammy like a melon
> He was drenched with gore
> He found himself curled up inside
> As if he had never been bore . . . (*C*, p. 77)

The poem brings Hughes's own interpretation of the legend into a light that shows the common spring of *Crow*, *Oedipus* and *Orghast*. The villain of the poem is related to St George, as told by Crow. He instructs Oedipus' father to clip shut Jocasta's vagina before the future patricide is born. Daddy (Laius) then tries to nip off his son's penis, so great is the fear of rival bodies imposed on him by his god. The son kills the father, then the Sphinx, that *god* has sent, no doubt at Daddy's request. The inside of the Sphinx releases ghosts in rotten bodies (diseased Thebans) as well as Daddy, who promptly kills Mammy, who then herself emerges from the Sphinx's guts only to be lopped in half by her son.

Seeing himself inside his mother's womb crowns the phallicist god's empire, so to speak, as Oedipus, through a growing enslavement to revenge reflex (urged on by the Sphinx, god's captive bait), gradually turns into a stillborn object fettered in the focus of a staring eye. A more distressing image of the total annihilation of affective life I cannot imagine unless it be Andy Warhol's projection of an electric chair, cut out of a mass-circulation newspaper, upon a disintegrating silk screen. Oedipus has placed himself at a point where imagination altogether ceases to function. He exteriorizes in all its repugnance exactly what one must – with the nearly inconceivable forces that require it – prepare oneself to accept, and that is perhaps the most primitive of instinctual censures which only *begins* with the preparedness to have sexual intercourse with one's own mother. Transforming instinctual life for such a preparedness describes accurately what Crow's horrific (to a normal, fully finished man) advocacy is all about. Generically, incest is *any desire* that St George or the god of the brain designates, that is, captures. I think one can understand now why some of the curses Crow was sent to lift made Hughes feel he was wandering into areas of the deepest kind of prohibition.

The final image of 'Song for a Phallus' sums up the resistance of the state which Crow is supposed to animate, by helping the poet who invented him to renew old organs and remake his body. Thus 'Song for a Phallus' is indirectly a sort of exorcism of the self at its worst. More positive action comes in a poem like 'Crow's Battle Fury' (C, p. 67). Here we see a self-as-object in the process of dying:

> One of his eyes sinks into his skull, tiny as a pin,
> One opens, a gaping dish of pupils,
> His temple-veins gnarl, each like the pulsing head of a
>   month-old baby . . .

One eye seems to telescope the full force of the outer world and its nearly unbearable cycles into the brain, while the other pops out like a hundred new ways to see the old world ('dish of pupils'): at the same time, with the image of 'temple-veins . . . of a month-old-baby', one understands that the old circuitry of the parietal lobes is being rewired. This re-organ-ization precedes Crow's first step, which can be taken only when dead organs are reformed and relations with inner and outer worlds are changed. Crow goes 'a hair's breadth out of the world', in meeting the brief given by the poet, to where perhaps un-nameable instinct can be imagined (i.e. can be known *without* the brain god, who would turn the 'knowledge' straight into taboo). Crow's first step welds the world to the re-organ-ized bird. This is the healing step akin to myth-making: a sensual imprint upon the world is like a sound resounding in the world's peritoneum. In short, Hughes has claimed a science-tinged body (referred to as 'the patient' in the poem), let it die, then reanimated it through Crow, whose imagination is required to transcend its own processes (much as a baby's imagination may be still controlled by basic cellular biochemistry); only then can the poet's advocate take a first, healing step.

The exorcism of the body-as-object and the subsequent mythic step are externalized in the narration of the penultimate double poem of *Crow*, 'Two Eskimo Songs'. The second of these is a lovely little tale about the same problem that was raised in 'Existential Song'. 'Fleeing from Eternity', the first song, tells of external man whose individual appearance in the physical world is defined as (a) having a face, a fixed emotional relationship with his surroundings, and (b) stealing spirit or song from woman, i.e. turning the eternal principle of renewal into a spiritless body, in exchange for which the woman is given the man's self-made face. This constitutes the tragedy which is answered in the following song, 'How the Water Began to Play'. Water wants to live; being an element essential to the life of other things is no good: 'It went to the trees [;] they burned [;] it came weeping back.' Water feels it lives vicariously, like the person at the end of 'Existential Song'. It keeps trying and trying till it wears itself completely out, 'Till it had no weeping left'. Only then does it, ironically, become what it is: neither a thing nor a part of a static, intransitive copula – not water *is* – but the essence of a *function* – water *being* – water lying 'at the bottom of all things / Utterly worn out   Utterly clear'.

The essential activity might, in turn, be said to define the perfect organ and the perfect organ-ism, which is no way self-regarding, which is worn out of every element that impedes transit, which is the pure *how* of things. The shark that crashed 'into the sea / And went downwards, discovering its own depth' ('Crow's First Lesson', C, p. 20) describes eloquently such an organism as well as the organism's relation to the world around it (that which is dived through). Such emphasis upon transitive action responds to the principal seductions of the sphinx, e.g. god's head-love religion ('"Love", said God, "Say, love",' C, p. 20). Constant transitive action mirrors Hughes's mythic activity, where naming is the gesture, the footstep – participation rather than a position. A hint of intransigence brings on the full spectrum of taboos and the real hell of Sisyphus' eternal motion. This is part of the point, however: new organs are rarely perfect and do not last long: 'We go on writing poems because one poem never gets the whole account right. At the end of the ritual up comes a goblin . . . within a week the whole thing has changed, one needs a fresh bulletin' (Interview I, p. 15).

*

Cave Birds (limited edition 1975; *Cave Birds: An Alchemical Cave Drama*, trade edition, 1978) ends with part of the quotation above, which expresses simply and clearly how and why Hughes writes. Retrieving the body, renewing the organ-ism, is a constant activity that recoils from a finished product, even more from a finished world. The new book represents a new 'bulletin' and new advocacy. A word about the peculiar textual history of this sequence – which more than *Crow* aspires to the status of a sequence – helps explain the long, non-sequential middle part.

In 1974, Hughes saw a score of pen and ink drawings by the American artist and one-time colleague of Sylvia Plath in 1957–8, Leonard Baskin. Using some of the drawings as touchstones, Hughes composed what became the first third and the two concluding poems of *Cave Birds* (1978). Hughes wrote a dozen more poems outside the initial sequence which Baskin answered with eight more drawings. Thus, in retrospect, there are three distinct stages in the building of the cave drama, which is why, between execution and rebirth ('The Accused', *CB*, p. 24 and 'The Risen' *CB*, p. 60), there is a very long limbo phase (17 out of the 29 poems).

In *Crow* Hughes said he used the story (if there is one) just as a mechanical sorter. I feel that the unity of a subjective quest is paramount in that book as it is also in *Cave Birds: An Alchemical Cave Drama*. But in *Cave Birds* there is a certain pretence of a logic of action which involves birth, 'The Scream', awareness, 'After the First Fright', 'The Interrogator', 'The Judge', 'The Plaintiff', 'The Executioner', a large number of middle-zone poems, then rebirth poems, 'Bride and Groom' – the liberated prisoner's epithalamium – and 'The Owl Flower' and 'The Risen'.

As the 'plot outline' perhaps suggests, Hughes's comments on Crow's need to recover and join up with God's prisoner, rather than destroy him, are pertinent for understanding the quest in *Cave Birds*. The task of the hero – a cockerel this time – who comes into the world of consciousness with 'The Scream', is again to disarm some sphinx who manifests herself in an accusing or staring aspect of Nature. This counter-attack consists, however, in dis-organ-izing the cockerel's self and then, with organs free from the fictitious 'ism' of their togetherness, in fully submitting to the eternal bride, the earth, under the one and only true covenant of spirit, the sun.

The cockerel's life begins with a scream vomiting *itself* out of his body (*CB*, p. 6). This first moment of conscious life confronts the autonomous presence of some instinctual cry outside the body. The cry, separate from self, is another sphinx, instinctual life trapped by some waking brain god. The cockerel that screams sees two things between his life as a happy, unaware child ('sun on the wall – my childhood's / Nursery picture') and death ('my gravestone / Which shared my dreams'): a mate, in the form of a body without brains, and the heads of calves on a counter, i.e. brains without bodies. Though this cockerel would instinctively like to praise all forms made by the 'wheel of the galaxy', he is stopped by the initial scream which goes on, in the poems that follow, to shore up its powers, as, often, old half-conscious fictions do. At this point in the sequence – really from the second or third poem on – we find ourselves in the by now familiar psychological territory of advocacy and sphinxhood. A part of a letter Hughes sent to Gifford and Roberts brings this terrain of the mind into a startling light:

> Part of the fascination of Hara-kiri is our recognition of what it implies – an ultimate confrontation of the real pain of pain, a deliberate, controlled translation of psychological pain into physical pain, the absolute acceptance of pain on its own terms. In that sense, it is an act not only of absolute courage, but of absolute honesty. It is *the* symbolic act of the acceptance of the *reality* of what hurts. It is part of the reverence – in that case not short of worship – for the actuality of inner experience. (*Study*, p. 260 – letters of October 1978 and October 1979)

Hughes is writing in response to a question asked about 'The Summoner' and 'After the First Fright' (*CB*, pp. 8, 10) especially with regard to the lines 'When I said: "Civilisation," . . . He disembowelled himself with a cross-shaped cut.' He wants to contrast genuine acceptance of the body that hara-kiri ritual requires and the sublimation of body that Christian images of crucifixion conjure up for the poet and his advocate, who is, like Crow, somewhat stupefied by the doctrine of love (especially in its humanized or in its platonized forms). The difference between hara-kiri and the Christian sacrifice is of central importance to what Hughes's protagonists must learn to accept or rehearse psychologically ('Oedipus Crow' (*C*, p. 43), 'Snake Hymn' (*C*, p. 87) and *Oedipus* all point towards the state of mind required for hara-kiri or – what amounts to the same thing – preparedness to have sexual relations with mother or sister, i.e. that experience where coextensiveness of body and world is most difficult mentally to accept). Total identity with body, when all censorious fictions or taboos are released, represents the basement door of Hughes's religious edifice, the 'new Holy Ground . . . that won't be under the rubble when the churches collapse' (Interview I, p. 19). Here, more than in *Crow*, there is a general, narrative movement towards this identity as the cockerel passes from confrontation with body deprived of a *raison d'être* ('The Interrogator') to a participation in the motor force of carrion-hood. Most poems up to 'The Owl Flower' can be read as self-conjurings that aim to dissociate the body from old fictions. The poet tells himself, through his advocate, that he is not a living being but a voyeur: 'The whole earth / Had turned in its bed / To the wall' ('In these Fading Moments', *CB*, p. 20). The earth, the untouched lover, confirms this silently but unequivocally. The executioner of the next poem (*CB*, p. 22) 'Fills up / Sun, moon, stars . . . With his hemlock', blotting out what little spirit is left in the random world of carrion. Here, with the mention of hemlock, one senses another drama, historical and concerned with a real, objective world that treats Socrates and the misfortunes (according to Hughes) of our own culture, so that a cultural as well as a personal renewal is hinted at. This cultural-historical dimension is admittedly slight and what there is of it is largely obscured by the limbo or middle poems.

However, the first idea of *Cave Birds* concerned 'the psychological crime, punishment and compensation of Socrates' (his death in 'The Executioner' being the cornerstone of western civilization's renunciation of body in favour of a Graves-type of Logos god). Hughes told Gifford and Roberts that the book was once subtitled

> The Death of Socrates and his Resurrection in Egypt – with some idea of suggesting that aspect of it which is a critique of sorts of the Socratic abstraction and its consequence through Christianity to us. His resurrection in Egypt, in that case, would imply his correction, his re-absorbtion into the magical-religious archaic source of intellectual life in the East Mediterranean, and his emergence as a Horus – beloved child and spouse of the Goddess. (*Study*, p. 260)

The perfect transformation of Rationalism, then, would be Oedipus and his culture's acceptance of incest, of lifting the ban on the coextensiveness of body from mother to child to other offspring. However, I think we can be grateful that Hughes followed his intuition and left the historical tableau to resonate psychologically. How the original idea would have meshed with the inner drama is difficult to imagine and, certainly, when Hughes once again felt the urge to 'move outwards' in this development, his writing poses genuine difficulties.

Cave Birds traces the cockerel's response to the Socratic brain god as he imitates the sort of anti-body, anti-fiction existence of Crow, for instance in 'The Knight' (*CB*, p. 28), one of the finest poems in the collection. The knight (here St George's opposite) excels at decomposition where Socrates excels at composing anything and everything into the mystifying dialectic of logic. This is how the knight outwits Socrates:

> The knight
> Has conquered. He has surrendered everything. . . .
>
>   He has conquered in earth's name.
> Committing these trophies
>
> To the small madness of roots, to the mineral stasis
> And to rain.

His 'submission is flawless' and, as 'blueflies lift off his beauty,' eventually nothing is left of the knight 'but his weapons / And his gaze.' Through him now the sun beams again, strengthening its 'revelation'. (Next to the poem is a drawing of a decomposed bird.) By the end of the poet's meditation, Socrates or Socrates' prisoner, body, has been set free: 'What is left is just what my life brought me / The gem of myself' (*CB*, p. 54). And the last three poems, 'Bride and Groom', 'The Owl Flower' and 'The Risen', march together superbly in regard both to the logic of the sequence and the subjective dedication to the ritual of marriage – to body which then gives way to rebirth. Hughes's epithalamium is a literal re-organ-ization: she gives him an eye, he gives her skin; she gives him teeth, he oils the movement of her mouth. The whole process is verified by the true spirit, the sun.

These last poems are perhaps responsible for the 1978 edition's sub-title, 'An Alchemical Cave Drama'. Hughes may have been thinking of Andrea's *The Chemical Wedding of Christian Rosencrantz* which, as early as 1964, inspired him to write a verse drama called 'Difficulties of a Bridegroom' (Interview II, p. 212). But, to me, the title in itself suggests, first, body and matter removed from the lights of anti-troglodyte types like Socrates (the cave – the earth's secret centre) and, second, a new, pure, mythic relationship to matter where the subject and his chemistry are of one and the same movement, matter and mind. The androgynous being put together in the grave (or cave), cheered on by real sun spirit – not human spirit – seems to grow radiant in the penultimate poem, 'The Owl Flower'. Here the eye, that elsewhere impales, acts as a source of energy, which sets inert body in motion. Hughes has completed a full ritual, giving an old body (for us readers, the sound itself of words) new vitality.

The emblem of achievement, a powerful hawk-like bird, a new cockerel perhaps, 'stands, filling the doorway / In the shell of earth . . . each wingbeat – a convict's release' (*CB*, p. 60). 'The risen' bird is miraculous for being a natural creature, *created by a poet*: the bird is a perfect mixture of matter and spirit so that, beneath its gliding wing, thickets in the shadow cry out for sun, or burst into flames to quench Nature's continuous need for spiritual (solar) infusion. 'The Risen' represents, then, the laborious hours that culminate in the uttering of the mythic copula verb, the naming of a new chemistry of poet and experience. Yet, just as soon as the poet's 'product', the precipitate of his chemical energy, hardens and tries to find lodging in the mind, the poet *must* move on. The question that closes the final poem and the sequence, 'But when will he land / On a man's wrist', sends us straight to the model of Sisyphus as mirror for the mind. There is no objective answer to Hughes's objective-sounding question, unless one imagines some sort of cultural devolution – not just back to Egypt and the rule of Isis, but back to the seamless world of the hominoid ape. (Do not most primitive people have clans? Is not Freud, in *Totem and Taboo*, in some sense right to adopt the totemism and taboo observance of primitive man as a basic model for modern man's neurosis?) As the book finally observes, after the ritual up comes the next goblin. The mythic copula is not *is* but the gerund of continual action, *being*. The bird will land on man's wrist as long as he continues to be made, in poetry or in some other way.

5

KEEPING FAITH WITH THE WORLD OF THINGS: 'GAUDETE', 'MOORTOWN', 'SEASON SONGS', 'REMAINS OF ELMET'

> Objective imagination, then, important as it is, is not enough. What about 'subjective' imagination? It is only logical to suppose that a faculty developed specially for peering into the inner world might end up as specialized as the faculty for peering into the outer one. . . . So what we need, evidently, is a faculty that embraces both worlds simultaneously. A large, flexible grasp, an inner vision which holds wide open, like a great theatre, the arena of contention, and which pays equal respect to both sides. Which keeps faith, as Goethe said, with the world of things and the world of spirits equally. (Myth II, pp. 91–2)

Cave Birds is not only loosely ordered by a narrative but also by poems that comment on each other through recurring images and encounters. More than *Crow*, it lays a claim upon that outside world which we can sense in the logic of action and in the self-criticism. Hughes's first prose or versicle novel, *Gaudete* (1977), makes this outside world appear primary. There is a plot that resembles a thriller or a detective story, with mass murder and lots of desultory sex. A wealth of connections between characters and symbols belie one's first impression – that Hughes has bungled a 'novel'. In fact, the desultoriness of almost all the action, like the collection of caricatures *it* animates, points to what seems the real centre of the book: as usual, to a second narrator's solicitations, through his advocate, to a sequestered body. From this point of view, *Gaudete* has the promise of being an astounding book. Yet the sheer amount of exterior detail, the urgency of the story and the large number of recognizable types (doctor, farmer, barmaid, Woman's Institute member, etc.) finally leave one with the feeling that the residue of some other work has intruded into the subjective drama. It is probable that the book's origins – it began as a script for a Swedish film director in the early 1960s – explain the division between a very visual, rapidly moving scenario and the psychodrama. The poems added as an 'epilogue' were part of a group of a hundred or so written in 1974–5 when Hughes feared he had cancer of the throat. Some of these 'charm' poems also went into 'Orts' (meaning refuse or remains of a flood) which forms part of the 'Earth-numb' section of *Moortown* (1979). This patchwork history may explain the difficulty of *Gaudete*, because one feels that Hughes treats people, places and institutions of a typical English village as nothing more than contemptible props in an exorcism.

The main body of the book is told by a silent narrator's surrogate who seems to undergo a kind of spiritual death in telling the story, thus making way for a new narrator, the reborn, profligate vicar who seems to be close in spirit and in earnestness to the mute *metteur en scène*. Yet the thought of the end of *Cave Birds*, that describes poetry as a continuous reaction to ever new goblins, makes us suspicious of any end to the narrator's advocacy. Myth-making, as it is continuous conversation with incessant demons, demands a continuous supply of personas – and this truth does not cease to hold in the 'Epilogue', with its misleading apocalyptic introduction. As suggested at the end of chapter 4, mythic naming involves in practice not only the copula *is* but the favourite gerund of the existential point of view, the gerund of transitiveness, *being*. With this comes that infinite multiplication of identities – one for every moment, one for every goblin – which drew both Kierkegaard and Camus to commend the impious renegade of Spanish Catholicism, Don Juan, the man with a thousand and more personalities.

Unlike Don Juan, the protagonist of *Gaudete*, the Reverend Nicholas Lumb, has but one personality which is tracked down and killed by a host of St George types, who discover, to their horror, that the priest has been copulating with every woman in the parish. The profligate vicar's escapades are preceded by a visit in which spirits take the real man into the underworld and replace him with an exact duplicate made from an oak log (the Reverend Lumb of the story):

This changeling proceeds to interpret the job of ministering the Gospel of love in his own log-like way.

He organises the women of his parish into a coven, a love-society. And the purpose of this society, evidently, is the birth of a Messiah to be fathered by Lumb. (*G*, p. 9)

At this point, 'The Argument' states, the spirits which created the love-mad Lumb 'decide to cancel him. . . . The result is that all the husbands of the parish become aware of what is happening to their wives' (*G*, p. 9). The story takes place on the day of this cancellation, the day Lumb dies. After his death, a chastened man (showing signs of the wounds inflicted by the outraged husbands) reappears in the west of Ireland, 'where he roams about composing hymns and psalms to a nameless female deity' (*G*, p. 9).

The advocate of the silent narrator, the force behind both the omniscient narration and the first-person persona of the poems of the 'Epilogue', is himself a double who sets his *alter ego*, the erotomaniac, in motion, then actually appears, in person, to try to stop his love-mad self (*G*, p. 77). Felicity, the secular bride of the would-be progenitor of the new Messiah, actually sees the real self trying to arrest his double. The same self returns in the shape of a bodiless hand extended over the shoulder of the profligate in his motor car (*G*, pp. 98 ff.), the very hand the *alter ego* had some hours earlier torn off his double and thrown into a lake. Moreover, the *alter ego*'s dreams – in the chapters 'Maude' (*G*, pp. 118–19) and 'The Cathedral' (*G*, pp. 121–3) – reveal the real link that the profligate's consciousness has all along maintained with the underworld which is responsible for the separation. There, amongst the dead, something is wrong – something with life in its death phase, that is, troubles the living. Through the split that has occurred in the narrator's own advocate, we understand *his* purpose, which in telling the story aims simply to reunify the world's three zones, of gods, of men, of the dead, in a voice that should sound finally undivided. The dispossession of the dead by the rest of life sparks off the advocacy and narration. The goal of the story-telling is like that of the rite of sinking the pole, *axis mundi* or Maypole, itself a form of sacred ash or ygdrasil, whose roots, trunk and branches tie the three strands of life into one. The Maypole is planted in the spring, at the end of an old world, a sick world of fruitlessness or of pestilence. At the beginning of *Gaudete*, before the zone of the living, Lumb, the *alter ego*, sees the Mother of death gravely ill: 'the woman tangled in the skins of wolves ... her face half-animal ... clear-dark back to the first creature ... animal cheekbone and jaw ... animal tendon in the turned throat'; she is a woman with a 'startling brilliant gaze' which 'knifes into' Lumb. (We begin again with Nature's imperious stare.) Next to her is a sad husband: 'who is the aged aboriginal crouching beside her; stroking her brow, stroking the hair off her brow ... with a trembling tenderness?' (*G*, p. 14). As in the beginning of *Orghast*, we see Moa and Sun divided, matter unspiritualized, spirit un-materialized. Lumb's quest begins here in this encounter. Next, he is showered with bull guts (a rite of bodily but not spiritual invigoration); then he enters his village with the idea of siring a new Messiah, an act analogous to the planting or blessing of the Maypole. But how can this be done by a brainless parson-body? As a physical hero, like Algoluz in *Orghast*, Lumb's body belongs to a fiction of profligacy of which he is only faintly aware. (Beneath the ground, his ego in the company of the ailing Goddess is fully aware.) One can understand his prayers to trees in this context: 'He tries to find in himself the muscle-root of prayer ... He tries to make this ash-tree his prayer' (*G*, pp. 52–3); 'And now embracing the tree he flattens himself closely into it. / With fixed imagination he sinks nerves into the current of the powerline' (*G*, p. 156).

These gestures suggest that the intellectual side of the physical hero's quest is a purely gnostic awareness of spiritual truth, i.e. truth not fleshed out in body or gesture but inert in mind. (Praying to trees is not the same thing as imitating the tree-powerline.) Lumb's goal is clearly explained by the grandfather of his secular financée, a rather surprising *porte-parole* (in the village pub) for vintage Hughesian Christianity, no doubt the religion the sickly couple below ground would like to see reinstated above:

> Christianity's something about women ...
> Christianity is Christ in his mammy's arms –
> Either a babe at the tit
> With all the terrible things that are going to happen to
>   him hovering round his head like a halo,

> Or else a young fellow collapsed across her knees
> With all the terrible things having happened. (*G*, p. 65)

So this is just the sort of wisdom Lumb is incapable of turning into reality. As his escapades reveal, this truth is equally lost on the village, whose members all live according to the same segregation of mind and matter that Lumb pushes to an extreme in his amorous exercises.

All men in the parish have suppressed their instinctual life, as can be seen in their relationship with women: GARTEN, who courts Felicity and who is said to plunder the underground with his pet ferret, looking for rabbits (*G*, p. 61); his compromising photographs of Lumb alert the other men to what is going on. HAGEN, who has turned the female deity into a deadly Männlicher (!) .318 rifle (he is also said to trade in pre-packaged bull sperm). The widower ESTRIDGE who is jealously possessive of his two nubile daughters, one of whom commits suicide, having grown pregnant through Lumb. Dr WESTLAKE, GP, objective student of the body and incredulous cuckold. HOLROYD, whom we see dehorning bulls. DUNWORTH, the architect and designer whose furniture is said to resemble 'demortalised organs of a body' (*G*, p. 130).

The female part of the village, Lumb's coven, consists of a good number of mindless Jocastas: Mrs EVANS, 'a viper' (*G*, p. 66) and the Woman's Institute secretary, who, when found out, says sex has 'nothing to do with loving the vicar' (*G*, p. 114). Mrs DAVIES, who is seen fornicating with Lumb on bags of peat in her nursery. Mrs GARTEN, ten years a widow, who has intercourse with Lumb next to crates full of rabbits (*G*, p. 68). The rest of the village women make up the harem, except for one, Maud, Lumb's caretaker.

Maud is the one woman Lumb does not make love to. We see her mainly in the role of an aloof servant. But Maud is the (ignored) female principle itself, in contact with the sickly woman we first met underground, whose message, rejoice, '*gaudete*', she reveals. But in Lumb's parish, no one will rejoice as long as matter and spirit are so divided. The collective female body of the village has been deprived of brains, whilst the male aspect, the mind, does not want the worm of life's death phase to do its work. 'The

92

representative in this world of the women [Lumb] is supposed to cure in the other world' (Interview II, p. 215), Maud is the abused and ignored centre of life. She is, for example, associated with a black and white bird, a magpie, when she communes with the dead in the cemetery near the rectory. The magpie tries to fly over the graveyard but is rebuffed by the wind. The passage of opposites – life in death, death in life – is impossible over the grave where Maud is seen arranging scattered shells, remnants perhaps of the original creation, a new creation or a homage to all that returns to its origins. After Lumb's mad pursuit by his double, which takes him through a muddy landscape of corpses and women flailing their arms, half buried, Maud is shown suckling a white dove, nurturing the spirit she knows her vicar does not have. When Lumb loses all signs of mental control, Maud tears the head off the bird, in an effort to control the vicar's body. And, in fact, soon after Lumb wanders to a vital area of communication with the triple world, to water: 'Sounds lump in his squeezed throat. / His lungs struggle, as under water' (G, p. 116). Maud attempts to direct Lumb to the part of life he neglects, by making water replace sounds. She is perhaps trying to teach him what true prayer might be. But when it becomes clear that Lumb is irredeemable, Maud becomes the deadly black widow who terminates the priest's career, denouncing him at the WI orgy where the new Messiah was supposed to be conceived.

Throughout the book we see Lumb's unconsious mind playing a role similar to Maud's, in his dreams and in his double's appearance. This double is often referred to as a water creature, a seal or otter. This image, like that of the triple Goddess Maud, the Maypole or ash tree, concerns the joining of several worlds. Like Maud, Lumb's double intervenes when the changeling pursues his relationship with Felicity. His strange presence, part physical and part psychical, takes us back to the one unifying person in the book, the silent narrator.

For it is clear that even the men of the village, Lumb's foes, are part of a silent narrator's projections, *projections against projections*, as a matter of fact. They are no more prepared than their vicar to submit to the eternal feminine, to their Maud. Lumb's death, then, is the destruction of one projection by another (just as *Cave Birds* is the ritual death of the cockerel that feeds God's prisoner, carrion or Nature deprived of spirit, and his rebirth as the fully spiritualized bird of 'The Risen'). Lumb's death makes Nature available, psychologically, to the silent narrator. This very narrator appears suddenly, with a new voice, in Ireland. He now seems to have the miraculous power of being able to control animals of the sea (an otter in fact). He leaves a sheaf of poems that a group of astonished young girls take to a Jesuit priest. Then the miracle worker goes about (or perhaps continues to go about) Ireland, writing poems to a nameless goddess.

In a way, we are prepared to expect the results of a kind of apotheosis akin to that at the end of *Cave Birds*, for the new Lumb can control the animal *par excellence* of the three kingdoms. What we get, instead, is an even more morose voice which continues to castigate itself for not living up to Nature's demands. Even now, after death and resurrection through water in Ireland, the writer of these 'hymns' (most sound like laments) is not a cubit nearer, psychologically, to the hara-kiri state of mind of complete submission. If anything, the poems sound more like a prologue to *Gaudete* than an epilogue, although it is true that all the lascivious bodies of the main narrative seem to have been exorcized. References to trees, which Lumb had earlier sought to emulate, still ring of desperate inadequacy (G, pp. 180, 183, 199). This is unfortunate because the 'Epilogue' contains some of Hughes's finest poems. But the tone of the speaker's voice, indeed the exact nature of his persona, are incompatible with the rest of the book. The poems are perhaps most profitably read on their own or in conjunction with 'Orts' in *Moortown* (M, pp. 132–49).

The two epigraphs to *Gaudete*, from Heraclitus and from Wolfram's *Parzifal*, address the subjective drama of the book pertinently. Heraclitus sees in the obscene songs and festivals, made in the spirit of Dionysus, an effective way of working out the mysteries of Hades, i.e. the mysteries of the body after death. Wolfram insists on finding God in life, denying neither the mystery of the after-life nor the pleasures of flesh. In Hughes's quotation, two brothers, one swart, the other fair, are fighting, unknowingly for the same end (the magpie which Maud sees blown backward over the graveyard rehearses a similar struggle). Joseph Campbell has glossed Wolfram's intention as follows, and it seems to me that his notes comment eloquently on the aim of the silent narrator of *Gaudete*:

> His own fanciful interpretation of his hero Parzival's name, *perce à val*, 'pierce through the middle,' gives the first clue to his ideal, which is . . . a realization here on earth, through human, natural means (in the sinning and virtuous, black and white, yet nobly courageous self-determined development of a no more than human life) of the mystery of the Word Made Flesh: the *logos* deeper than logic, wherein dark and light, all pairs of opposites — yet not as opposites — take part.

In Wolfram's own words, as translated by Professor Campbell: 'A life so lived that God is not robbed of the soul through the body's guilt; yet can retain with honor the world's favor: that is a worthy work' (*Creative Mythology*, pp. 431–2).

The workings of the subjective drama in *Gaudete*, on their own, make the book extraordinary and rich. At the same time we have to be prepared simply to ditch a lot of the simple, sensuous material of place, character and action to appreciate the book's unity and purpose, which is more of a psychological chant of *contemptus mundi* than any attempt to keep favour with the world (as Wolfram's advocate is careful to remember). Hughes's later works in fact seem quite conscious of this neglected side of grace, as can be seen in the quotation from 1976 at the head of this chapter. Unfortunately, when applied to *Gaudete* (as Hughes himself does in the quotation from Wolfram), the comment about a faculty which embraces both worlds simultaneously, which keeps faith 'with the world of things and the world of spirits equally', is simply wishful thinking.

Compared to Hughes's other books of poetry, *Moortown* (1979) comes closest to being just an anthology of unrelated parts. It consists of several sequences and a grouping of separate poems. All sections of the book appeared in limited editions before 1979 (though often longer and with variants): 'Prometheus on his Crag', which goes back to work on *Orghast* in 1971, came out in 1973; 'Orts' in 1978; 'Moortown Elegies' in 1978 and 'Adam and the Sacred Nine' in 1979. The section 'Earth-numb' reprints 'The Lovepet' from the American edition of *Crow* (1971) as well as a poem first published as early as 1963, 'Heatwave'.

Despite the varied sources, one feeling recurs more than any other in the volume as a whole, and that is *numbness*. Hughes told Keith Sagar, for example, that he regarded 'Prometheus on his Crag' as being a 'limbo . . . a numb poem about numbness' (*Art*, p. 147). Referring to the title poem of 'Earth-numb' (*M*, pp. 95–6), Hughes said, in his Norwich Tapes recording, 'the title refers to the strange unconscious sort of consciousness in which, it seems to me, all hunting and angling operations take place'. This sort of numbness in the waking mind is perhaps the quarry of 'Moor-town Elegies' which Hughes introduces with the following remarks:

> It's extremely difficult to write about the natural world without finding your subject matter turning ugly. In that direction of course lie the true poems, the great complete statements of the world in its poetic aspect – I mean that catalogue of disasters and miseries, *The Book of Job*, or that unending cycle of killings and grief, *The Iliad*, or the great tragedies. What all those works have in common, of course, is not exactly a final, up-beat note, but it is a peculiar kind of joy, an exaltation. But that's the paradox of poetry, as if poetry were a biological, healing process: it seizes on what is depressing and destructive and lifts it into a realm where it becomes healing and energizing. (NT)

Exaltation, numbness, a peculiar form of consciousness: all describe pretty much the same frame of mind needed to participate mythically in experience, to be on the same 'wavelength' as Nature's 'consciousness' or energetic process.

The story of *Orghast*, reported in chapter 4, puts one in the picture for 'Prometheus on his Crag'. The sequence is a fine one, perhaps not as closely knit as the best group of poems in *Moortown*, the 'Seven Dungeon Songs', but it is none the less loaded with 'sphinx' psychology (here, the vulture). Poem 20, 'Prometheus on his crag / Pondered the vulture' is one of the most lucid of the group. The eternal consciousness, aware of the mortal body's eternal pains, asks: is this circling, cyclical bird 'his unborn self' or 'his condemned human ballast'; 'his anti-self – / The him-shaped vacuum / In unbeing' or 'the Helper / Coming again to pick at the crucial knot / Of all his bonds' (*M*, pp. 90–1)? The questions disclose revealing aspects of Prometheus' relationship with the body which the bird can endlessly torture. As the final lines of poem 20 suggest: 'Image after image. Image after image. As the vulture / Circled / Circled.' – the point is that any image sublimates the body. The vulture-as-image is the trap for the body, which should never be allowed to become fiction, even the *hero* of fiction. It must simply be submitted to in a state of mind consonant with that of hara-kiri or 'numbness'.

The tailpiece of the sequence works with volcanic imagery as if the acquisition of this state of mind by Prometheus had turned his rock and his dilemma into a vigorous telluric revival. Here, with words that stretch the mind's eye to its limit ('the cloudy bird / Tearing the shell / Midwifes the upfalling crib of flames', *M*, p. 92), Prometheus is freed from his mother's eyes (the origin of the body-fiction), then begins to 'tred', making his first full, transitive active gesture which binds him to sensory experience (the feel of the new earth).

This is precisely the gesture at the end of a sequence related to 'Prometheus', 'Adam and the Sacred Nine': 'The sole of a foot / Pressed to world rock, flat warm' is a primordial gesture of contact Adam makes with virgin earth, never touched since it was 'star-blaze': 'I was made / For you' (*M*, p. 170). This is the first footfall, the 'tred' at the end of 'Prometheus'. In contrast with Prometheus, Adam, at the beginning of the sequence, has already dropped out of the fully spiritualized world and lies 'low as water' (*M*, p. 160), rather like water at the end of 'How the Water Began to Play' ('Utterly worn out   utterly clear', *C*, p. 93). Adam in fact is not only just himself, worn out of otherness, but is totally resistant to the various forms of action visited upon him by the 'sacred nine' birds. He is pure spirit, psychologically in a state of gnosis, that cannot lift a finger. Only through embodiments of spirit is he finally moved to the simple act that is also a marriage to the world's body which, *itself*, has been deprived of Adam's light. As may be intuited, the play of perspectives here is at once subtle, suggestive and confusing.

For the play of perspectives, themselves part of what is at once a cosmogony, a little Genesis and man's psychological relationship to this story of origins, the short sequence 'Seven Dungeon Songs' (*M*, p. 123–8) is unrivalled in its outer and inner continuity. And yet, looking back to 'The Hawk in the Rain', one can see here a poem which is, in essence, almost identical to this early narration of man's relationship with the natural world. But certainly, the songs are more complex, the narrative voice more extensive and the voices of lesser and greater selves less accessible.

The poem tells of the Fall, in which man is separated from the created world. What follows is an interiorized attempt at re-integration with the world. The narrator himself is the prisoner of the Dungeon, which has been erected by a god very much like the God of Logos as described by Robert Graves. His quest is, indirectly through the making of the poem, directly by achieving a certain state of mind, to have the earth *speak* him, i.e. to be recreated as an unmediated vocable of the natural world, freed from the tyranny of mind or rather of the mind's destructive fictionalizations of the body.

The first poem tells of our origins. In the beginning a wounded wolf with gangrenous breath gazes down at a gurgling 'soft-brained' baby, picks it up and runs into the stars, leaving, from its dripping tits, a milky way, a galaxy, behind. The milk suggests the nutrient matter of the created world, as it is available to man in his suckling stage. But the milk comes from a dying animal, said to be a 'pretty creature' to the man-child, who apparently enjoys a close relationship with the animal; the wolf's sickness is communicated almost automatically, through its 'gangrenous breath', to the young 'tabula rasa' of a child. Thus man, at the very outset, is shown to be born with, or to inherit early on, a diseased relationship with the mother and the building matter of the cosmos. As the wolf scatters her milk in the heavens, man is left behind to cry 'among the precipices' of a world where the mother element is first sick, then dead. Hughes is saying that our earliest memories which are capable of coming into contact with the blank sheet of infancy either recreate there the disease of the species (through the act of recollection) or discover there an infant who has already carried out its own, personal Cartesian clearing of the decks of sensory experience, in favour of ideas.

In the second song, wounded mother earth has died and become 'space-earth', Nature that goes on ticking while man, her murderer, lives outside and without her. Yet, like a vampire of brain, man, 'reckless of blood', sucks the life out of Nature's offspring, leaving behind dead, spiritless matter and a physical world stunned by clichés and other familiar human fictions: 'leaving names / Being himself nothing' – nothing but a monstrous segregating force. The rising god of this motherless world is:

> What it is
> Risen out of mud, fallen from space
> That stares through a face. (*M*, p. 124)

That is, the god is a head that has grown out of dust, yet which traduces, with a face, simple sensuality: instead of a smile, a grimace or tears, man is essentially what 'stares through a face', what transcends immediate sympathetic reactions, like the knitted brow that belies sly brain waves.

Having pictured god, Hughes returns, in the third song, to the earth, to body. The narrator of this poem seems to be conscious of the curse which the brain god has brought to earth. He wants to reassemble and reanimate the material world that is basic and sovereign – where the brain god's world is exclusive and self-made. The 'I' of this song wants to bring spirit to the seemingly least animate of things, the stone. But this 'I', it turns out, owns a body ruled by the brain god. His efforts are frustrated ultimately by what must be called the brain god within him, in short by self-consciousness:

> Only still something
> Stared at me and screamed
> Stood over me, black across the sun,
> And mourned me, and would not help me get up.
> (*M*, pp. 124–5)

This consciousness of a more genuine kind of consciousness – the sun itself – is the real demon, and the fact that this self-consciousness is not just anti-spirit but pure spirit commingled with and captured by brain god spirit makes union with the earth's original vital spark all the more difficult.

The fourth song treats the difficulty of restoring this union in man. Psychologically, this is the most complex of the seven songs. With the 'I' having just failed to reassemble himself, body and spirit, the ancient, pre-brain god of energy manages somehow to make its way into the earth's crust (out of which man is made but which man, the partner of the brain god, has also perverted). Light creeps through to quicken the dead, to bring spirit to what the brain god has rendered chaotic and elemental. The light that gets through the earth (and thus to man's chaotic body) is called 'Earth's halo'. To me, this suggests a concept of matter that has, so to speak, sprung a leak, a concept that allows vital spirit to subsist in spite of itself. (The normal role assigned to the concept is to drive out this spirit.) 'Earth's halo', for the same reason, makes one think of a concept of something difficult if not impossible to conceptualize, something that has an insubstantial objective existence. Translated into psychological terms, all this means that rational man, the partner of the brain god, may, in a moment when his reason springs a leak, fail to account for everything, be caught unawares by some spontaneous spirituality, some joy or *élan*, which may help him throw off the chain-mail system of thought that separates him from the natural world. But, by the end of this song, the brain god is back at work, wakened from his short nap, plugging up the holes that have let sunshine and air enter the earth. Like Krogon who becomes ever more desperate with each new generation of his offspring, the brain god here seems frenetic and desperate, as he gulps up air to ensure that the earth stays suffocated. Sucking up the air he is afraid will penetrate the surface, his lips resemble 'an eye to a crack'. Like the face which is nothing but 'a stare through' for furtive brain waves, the sensual contour of god's face here is determined by the principle of denying potentially living matter what it needs to live. Here is the particular quality, then, of the brain god's stare: his vacuum-like lips are his organ of sight, the exact opposite of solar 'vision' (or 'crowcolour'), which beams down warmth. The brain god pulls in and imprisons everything he sees. Unlike the 'Tree of Light' mentioned in the poem, the brain god's task is to keep the various realms of the world strictly separated: no animating spirit here, linking heavens, earth and the underworld.

Song 5 focuses on the inheritor of the long chain of atavism in which man, the partner of the brain god, grows more and more cunning in stopping light from entering the earth or spontaneous joy from affecting his own constitution. This is the creature, as Hughes has written, with two distinct nervous systems. The more one tries to reconcile the two, the worse things become: 'I look for people with clever fingers / Who might undo me ... People's fingers snarl it worse.' This is why the inheritor dances 'The dance of unbeing'.

In song 6, the subject raised is the possibility that in the outside world, outside the hopeless inheritor, there might be some moral instruction, some 'oracle'. But it soon becomes clear that if this exists then man's organs are too confused or enervated to make any use of it:

> The human eyes, jammed in flesh,
> Which seemed to know, in their silence,
> Were graves
> Of silence. (*M*, p. 127)

Even if the outer world is taken in sensually, its message is of such dimensions as to underscore again the irony of the nervous systems in song 5. In song 6 the image of some ancient, menhir-like stone, 'the tall rock of the sacred place' seems now to serve as a contumacious memento to what memory cannot recall or understand. The stone is perhaps part of a more ancient, earth/man language, too organic in its symbolism to be understood by the present-day mind.

This image leads directly to the central message of the whole sequence of songs which concerns imprisonment and the making of words. Song 7 is built like a chant or a prayer, upon parataxis: 'If mouth . . . If ear . . . If eyes . . .' The focus that such a prayer brings to the sequence is startling for, suddenly, we realize that the first six poems have in fact been a kind of internal or psychic drama of the Creation, the Fall and the Quest. Prayer, here, is not directed at or for anything so much as it serves, thanks to its repetitiveness, to put the narrator himself into a special frame of mind, no doubt akin to the 'hallucination in the streaming air' that is the sight of the hawk, or generally, 'numbness' before the natural world. Song 7 makes the earlier poems, taken together, appear as an inner drama of exorcism, whose goal is to act out, rehearse and dispel a cunningly established curse (exteriorized in the behaviour of the brain god). What the narrator in the prayer now asks for objectively – in the recurring invocations of his chant that subjectively serves to bring on the new state of mind – is nothing less than new organs and a new body to accommodate what the brain god, his ego, contrives so skilfully to deny.

Objectively, the apotheosis of the tragic person seen dangling and dancing the dance of unbeing, in song 5, would occur when, in the words of song 7, the world itself 'Might speak me'. Only in loosening the old animal body from the new human brain, the sensuous sounds from the intellectual meaning, can the mythic act of naming, or rather of inducing the earth itself to name one's own self, begin. What would be spoken would no doubt resemble the oracle language of menhirs and dolmens, except that the body would be the earth's vocables; its organs would be its grammatical parts and its whole being, its statement. This language would resemble a perfected kind of *Orghast* speech perhaps. At all events, what 'Seven Dungeon Songs' acts out and tries subjectively to induce is simply the mythic copula 'I *am*' – which, uttered by the world, couples man and world, like Prometheus' first transitive active gesture or Adam's foot pressed to earth rock, in the perfect continuum (both linguistic and existential) 'world *is/am* I'. Here, as one can detect, the subjectivity is even more radical than in other sequences. The new self is not a phoenix, but, if such nuances can be made, the (existential and grammatical) object of the subject, world. This is perhaps just a way of emphasizing a new identity through the loss of a previous identity. For some readers this nuance may lie beyond the spectrum of what is intelligible.

'Seven Dungeon Songs' is however one of the great, heroic sequences of *Moortown*. It is placed, unfortunately, in the most uneven and perhaps sloppy section of the book, 'Earth-numb'. The title poem is, none the less, a gem ('Earth-numb', *M*, pp. 95–6) and also a crystal ball for Hughes's next enterprise, *River* (1983): here the poet has more than anywhere else and quite possibly for the first time managed the fidelity to outer and inner he speaks of in his essay on myth quoted from at the beginning of this chapter. Always remaining true to the stages of catching his salmon, Hughes succeeds also in tracing the process by which one grows 'earth-numb', or hooked on one's own prayer for a fish, a prayer which has the same power over the salmon as the power of a faith healer or witch doctor can exert over his patient:

> The lure is a prayer. And my searching –
> Like the slow sun.
> A prayer, like a flower opening.

The natural world, with its guiding 'mind', the sun, aligns itself with the angler's lure, itself a literal extension of self-induced allurement. The fish is first 'electrocuting malice'. Then, 'A piling voltage hums jamming me stiff' (*M*, p. 95). As distinct from Lumb's prayer, the fisherman's lure-prayer seems to unite the three kingdoms ('through me / From river to the sky, from the sky to the river') in a way that is both psychologically and sensually right (the play of water depths, surface, sun and reflection). Yet the real *coup de fion* is still to come as the prize for being earth-numb is won. The poet's mind is reflected in his catch, the 'wagging stone pebble head / Trying to think on shallows' which dies just as the angler's spell of magic that has brought man and fish together wanes, and then gags 'on emptiness / As the eyes of incredulity / Fix their death-exposure of the celandine and cloud' (*M*, p. 96). One can look at this poem, without fear of deception, from the opposite angle, as the coruscation that rises up through the water's pure-thinking depths, palpitating to the movement of its fish lungs, deprived by a magician (the fisher) in a moment of confidence, of its flickering force. 'Earth-numb', the poem, opens up vistas hardly known in Hughes's poetry which happily continue into the life and shores of *River* (1983).

Certainly the larger part of the section 'Earth-numb' lets one down, at times appallingly, as in the six poems after 'Earth-numb', all of which are palpably and artificially rhetorical. Many of the poems from 'Orts' clearly belong with the end of *Gaudete*: 'Each new moment my eyes' (*M*, p. 132) is nearly the same poem as 'Trying to be a leaf' (*G*, p. 180) or 'What will you make of half a man' (*G*, p. 176). 'Grosse Fuge' (*M*, p. 136) recapitulates 'Music, that eats people' (*G*, p. 182), and 'The Cathedral' (*M*, p. 137) stands in uncomfortable proximity to 'Churches topple' (*G*, p. 190). All told, the twenty-five poems in 'Orts' are some of the weakest of a genre and a perspective of which Hughes elsewhere proves himself to be the undisputed master – with strong competition coming only from a poet like Rilke.

'Moortown', the sequence, claims to be simply a diary of Hughes's farming experience with his father-in-law, Jack Orchard, in mid-Devon. In feel, it has a texture and an informality that links it directly to an earlier book, *Season Songs* (limited edition 1974, USA edition 1975, UK edition 1976). In fact, three poems, 'Sheep 1 and 2' and 'March Morning Unlike Others' from *Season Songs* are reprinted in 'Moortown'. The two sequences differ quite a bit in their relationship to the conditions that usually prevail in Hughes's psychodramas, in the sense that the 'dual fidelity' to a sensuous world and to a world of spirits seems suddenly to lose the acutely problematic quality that pervaded *Gaudete*. For a reason that must be accepted as self-evident, man is at home in the natural world, a midwife to the natural processes, bringing lambs into the world or terminating the lives of those suffering, unable to quit the womb. Too naturalistic to be pastorals or eclogues, occasionally georgic in so far as they show the ways and instruct in the techniques of country life, most 'Moortown' poems are bound to evoke a great variety of reactions. Some readers will feel like participants in a strange, new world; others will find, as I do, most of the poems intolerably flat. Only the last few poems in the sequence fix a recognizable tone – that of elegy – to celebrate and mourn the life and passing of Jack Orchard.

Compare the bloody dreams of 'Hawk Roosting' (*L*, p. 26) with 'Poor Birds':

> Poor birds
> In the boggy copse . . .
> All night . . .
> They dream the featherless, ravenous
> Machinery of heaven . . . (*M*, p. 19)

In 'Poor Birds' a human perspective is allowed almost to connive with the birds, where, in the roosting hawk's mind, half the force concerns the way Nature works, the other the way man does not work. There is tension and drama in the latter, flaccid sympathy in the former. 'Dehorning' in 'Moortown' (*M*, pp. 17–18) is near to a georgic mode (and will be of interest to readers contemplating farming cattle). Compare, however, the pathos of the same operation in *Gaudete* (*G*, pp. 126–7) where it stands for a mindless sacrilege of body.

The year's cycle informs the movement of *Season Songs*, 'Moortown' and *River* (the latter two covering about fifteen months and one year respectively). The poems written to Jack Orchard, another 'Dick Straightup' (*L*, pp. 17–19) or human ygdrasil, are the best of the section because of the depth of characterization which brings alive both a rough-and-ready farmer and an obedient servant of the Goddess. The rough hands of labouring in 'A Memory' and 'Now You Have to Push' (*M*, pp. 63, 65) become, at the end of 'Hands', eloquent of a deeper female presence, as though suddenly death revealed the hands to belong to a midwife, indeed to a mother:

> Your hands lie folded, estranged from all they have done
> And as they have never been, and startling –
> So slender, so taper, so white,
> Your mother's hands suddenly in your hands –
> In a final strangeness of elegance. (*M*, p. 68)

The elegy, whose purpose it is to search out something enduring in a turbulent and transitory setting, almost seems here to embrace the sentiment of the classical ecstasy of pastoral tradition (like Donne's) or the exequy (like Lord Herbert of Cherbury's 'An Ode upon a Question Moved, Whether Love Should Continue for Ever?' or Henry King's 'The Exequy'). What is common to all is a movement towards hermaphroditism, an invocation of a zone or a sentiment where sexuality retreats to changelessness, where the female becomes visible in the dying male, or the two merge as conscious-perfect motors of change.

Besides *River*, the closest companion-piece to the achievement of the poem 'Earth-numb' is the collection *Remains of Elmet* (1979) which was written around the time when the 'Moortown' sequence was composed, in 1977. The poems are accompanied by high contrast black-and-white photographs by Fay Godwin. The accomplishment of the book lies in the extraordinary play of memory and response between the older poet and the young lad in his favourite childhood haunts. Deeper than personal memory, Hughes's recollection aims to flesh out an ancient, pre-industrial folk memory with a view to reviving the 'last Celtic Kingdom' – the Kingdom of Elmet – which begins for the adult in his dead family, childhood fishing trips, the awful Rock, the body-hating Mount Zion chapel, the whole length of what he recalls as 'the hardest-worked river in England' (*RE*, p. 8). The kingdom which memory resurrects may not be a new Egypt ruled by Isis, mother of the gods, but it is full of seductive poems which lead in this direction.

Comparing several poems associated with Heptonstall, where Sylvia Plath is buried – 'Heptonstall' from *Wodwo* (*W*, p. 165), 'Heptonstall Cemetery' and 'Heptonstall' (*RE*, pp. 122, 92) – one sees in the first a sad, defenceless poem about a gravestone village; in the second, a gentle calling upon Sylvia, mother, father and uncle, to come live in words; in the third a quest to recover Ariadne's clew and travel through the labyrinth of mental distance and time to the nearly abandoned land around Heptonstall, where neighbours are rare and visitors to dead neighbours even more infrequent. Hughes pictures in this worn-out, post-industrial Heptonstall a lonely, arthritic man, disconnected from the community, encircled ironically by telegraph wires through which time moans 'its amnesia'. The poem becomes, gradually, an act of retrieval as the old man's leaking mind is gathered into verse, itself a turning of words on older words, leading recollection into its memorial which is also a loving embrace, a transfusion from a dying mind and from disintegrating perceptions – 'the broken circle of the hills / Drift apart' – to a living one. Many similar poems are like fishing trips, requiring the same earth-numbness to bring the hidden salmon, history, to the shore.

Remains of Elmet is of a piece, one memorial feeling which – uncharacteristically for Hughes – brings two 'objective' aspects of life, history and real place, together mythically with the writer, whose poetry is at times close to an exalted form of remembering. Beneath the surface of what this memory uncovers, we see enduring traces of Egypt, Hindustan and Asia Minor ('Willow Herb', Hardcastle Crags', *RE*, pp. 73, 13, and 'The Ancient Briton Lay under His Rock', *RE*, p. 84), despite the intervention of Calvin and Wesley ('Mount Zion' and 'When Men Got to the Summit', *RE*, pp. 82, 56), the concomitant flight from the land (for Hughes, from Nature itself – in 'Dead Farms, Dead Leaves', *RE*, p. 55) and the blasting of the valley ('The Canal's Drowning Black', 'The Long Tunnel Ceiling', *RE*, pp. 74, 76–7).

By making his tribe's memorial, constructing the Englishman's new Stonehenge, reinstating the Kingdom of Elmet – all this is a book that sets out with modest ambitions, to provide a commentary for a collection of startling photographs – Hughes shows perhaps another route to the freeing of the body, a gentler, 'Orphic' route, where one accepts without pride or outrage that the journey is more valuable than the goal, that brass can be burnished as well as fought with.

6

CONCLUSION: 'WHAT IS THE TRUTH?', 'RIVER'

The aim of this book has been to emphasize the drama and the gestures behind the 'verbal surface' of Ted Hughes's poetry. At the same time I wished to steer reactions away from concepts like poetic 'themes' and 'motifs' and concomitant impressions of violence (or gritty vigour) and direct attention instead towards a subjective point of view sensitive to the needs that cause the poetry to be written in the first place. As such, the poetry is first of all exorcism – aimed at disassembling a number of taboos or sphinxes – and then it is myth, in so far as body and instinctual life are freed and re-assimilated by the self. I have said that this drama of exorcism is painful and tricky because its quarry, the monster or anti-self, is as powerful as the intimate reflexes and feelings of the self he controls are intense. Moreover, I wanted to show that the impression that the inner drama is ever-recurring or continuous (thus is, objectively, absurd) reflects the subjective point of view of myth-making, which passes from a relative to a totally subjective point of view where subject, body and world are indistinguishable. I called the goal of Hughes's poetry *being*, in this sense: that is, perpetual, transitive activeness.

If, in doing all this, I have managed to construct a door to Hughes's world, then I hope at least it is left sufficiently ajar to let one see how subtle his work is psychologically, mythically and existentially. As Hughes has said of others, writers elect instinctively to develop either towards an inner world or towards an outer world of sensuous or ideal realities – of things, people, history or politics. Recently, Hughes's own literary itinerary has changed a good deal, and I shall look at this, in *River*, shortly. But until 1979 Hughes's path (that of greatest interest anyway) had led in one direction only: inwards – sometimes, in the early poetry and, more ambiguously, in *Gaudete*, inwards as though in spite or anger.

Each reader will no doubt have a different feeling about the extent of inwardness and the results that flow from his quest. When the poet wrote in 1976 of the need for a faculty that embraces both inner and outer worlds simultaneously, which keeps faith, as Goethe said, with both the world of things and the world of spirits, he may well have been thinking about an evolution in his own art which was just beginning, and which comes to the fore in the diary poems in 'Moortown'. In a subjective poetry like Hughes's, there must be a point where exorcism and ever-recurring goblins (which deliver the ever-changing 'bulletin' to the poet) make one think less of myth-making and being than of mirror reflections and subjective perceptions. There must be, that is, a point where, for every intuition experienced by a superior self, a lesser or goblin self exists, between whose internalized warfare the poet is gradually worn down to a frazzle. At such a moment one will sense Self rather than Vision in the hawk's eye, and pride in the hierophantic denunciation of the lesser self's pride, the confidence or certainty of some *homme moyen sensuel*. There will be a faint sense of *hubris* in the iconoclasm, the weight of one's person rather than Nature in the Sisyphean rock.

The dangers of being victimized by the vicious play of mirrors, of self and anti-self, or by some perception bigger than imagination or intuition itself (which yields virtually the same result), have never concerned Hughes consciously in his work. Some of the least unfair negative criticism has, however, aimed roughly in this direction, at these dangers of Jekyll and Hyde attrition. More often than not, though, the objections have not been part of criticism as a mode of discourse, but part, quite simply, of an opposing fiction – usually realistic and humanistic – which values both the sensual world and the activities of the same *homme moyen sensuel* which Hughes distrusts.

Here I should like to say one final word about the conditions of

Hughes's fiction which this 'criticism', though uncomprehending, is right to attack or feel worried about, in so far as it is argued from a different intuition of values. I think that this well-known passage by the Elizabethan poet Sir Philip Sidney shows exactly why the double-edged sword of salvation gets sharpened (both to repair and to wound) even though the intention is to abolish the sword altogether:

> Neither let it be deemed too saucy a comparison to balance the highest point of man's wit with the efficacy of nature; but rather give right honour to the heavenly Maker of that maker, who, having made man to his own likeness, set him beyond and over all the works of that second nature: which in nothing he showeth so much as in poetry, when with the force of a divine breath he bringeth things forth far surpassing her doings, with no small argument to the incredulous of that first accursed fall of Adam, since our erected wit maketh us know what perfection is, and yet our infected will keepeth us from reaching unto it. (*An Apology for Poetry*)

For all the persuasiveness about man being virtually a Maker made by the Maker, absolutely nothing can defuse the fact of Adamic history and infected will. Sidney's cresting wave of humanism is erected by nothing other than some accursed undertow. Whatever one says – and Sidney says about as much as can be said – about the powers of the creative eye, the fact is that aprons (Gen. 3:7) first existed to cover up what *should not be seen*. In the Judaeo-Christian tradition, and even here in this attempt to mix in humanism, the tree of knowledge has a canonical status in *existence* – not in epistemology or wit. Wit is above all the opposite of the goblin anti-self, infected by will, and in the service of poetry it is more an exorciser than a creator and redeemer. Hughes's heroes – Sostris in *Orghast*, Prometheus, Crow and the cockerel of *Cave Birds* – are all solicited by a 'cursed' poet to serve for him as advocates of an anti-curse. Sidney's unhappy lover, Astrophel, hard-hit, despite his better sense, by appetite ('"But ah," desire still cries, "give me some food"'), is pre-eminently the poet's advocate against the curse of voyeurism, censured, sensual vision or, simply, knowledge. He is hardly a free spirit before a virginal, unknown, mute and bare world (as in humanist or idealist models of epistemology, like those of Bruno or Kant or Wallace Stevens). What Sidney's comments help to clarify, in a language somewhat 'closer to home', is that once the spectre of pre-existence or pre-historic tragedy is evoked – appetite or infected will for Sidney, the parietal lobes and a legion of sphinxes for Hughes – the only way to escape fully from the mixed results of repetitive exorcism is quite simply to turn one's back on Adam and reject the adequacy, as a basic truth, of the Fall. Only after this *can* the maker assert himself as a true knower, a person for whom knowledge *is* making , rather than exorcism of a knowing knower or a seductive self-conscious maker.

Since 'Moortown' and *Season Songs* a new mood, powerful enough to deflect the many devious atavisms of the goblins-of-the-lobes, seems to have been moving into the ascendant, though still mixed at times with the old psychodrama. This queer coexistence can be felt in the collection 'Earth-numb' where sequences like 'Adam and the Sacred Nine' or 'Seven Dungeon Songs' are found next to much more naturalistic, descriptive poetry. The remarkable synthesis of a poem like 'Earth-numb', where spiritual and sensuous truth mix so well, is relatively rare until *River* (1983). In a sense, therefore, Hughes's most recent book (aimed at young readers – 'a farmyard fable for the young'), *What is the Truth?* (1984), has many of the problems of mixed tones or mixed modes which *River* had seemed to solve. More than the mixing, however, the major problem in *What is the Truth?* is the rhetoric of the different elements in the story, the relation between them or, more precisely, how the reader understands the various elements. Here is the book's setting as described on the dust cover:

'We will speak to the people,' said God. 'We will ask them a few simple questions. Then you shall hear. In their sleep they will say what they truly know.'

It is two o'clock in the morning, and God and his son look down from a grassy hilltop on the spire and roofs of a village. Summoned in their sleep, the inhabitants one by one describe truly an animal they know well. Among the describers are the Farmer, his Wife and Son, the Vicar, the Poacher, and the Shepherd; among the described are the Fox, the

111

Badger, the Cow, the Sheep ... and many other animals and birds. The descriptions take the form of poems ...

The allegory is something like the story of Jesus or of Samuel Johnson's *Rasselas*, in which a prince who lives in a perpetually happy valley escapes to see how the other half live. Declining his Father's advice – 'Curiosity is dangerous. Be satisfied with Heaven' (*WT*, p. 9) – the son comes down to the hillside where God calls up the souls of the village folk who tell their stories ('When they are asleep, they are widest awake', *WT*, p. 9).

Thus, what we read is bound to be understood to a certain degree as both an inquisition of the unguarded self (by God) and a dialogue between ordinary mortals and their better self in the person of the son of God, who is listening in with us. The first problem arises when we notice that some poems are lovely, naturalistic evocations of the created world, while others are quite intense psychodramas which already include a subtle dialectic of voices and selves. Here, for instance, is a beautiful evocation of a sheep:

> The Sheep is a small inland sea,
> A wave on four legs,
> A living foam, with a heart for a fish
> And blood of real sea-water, and half-moon eyes.
>
> The Sheep is a mobile heaven, it nibbles the hill,
> A manageable cloud,
> A cloud for a lawn, or a field-corner.
> A small, patient cloud
> In whose shade the Shepherd's dog can rest.
> A cloud going nowhere,
> Growing on the hillside, fading from it –
> A cloud who teaches quiet. (*WT*, p. 41)

The last of the book's tales concerns a Schoolteacher (the narrator), his hunter friend from Australia, and their quarry, the fox. The story recreates much of the effect of 'Earth-numb'. In the Schoolteacher's poem, it is the 'hunter's magic' (*WT*, p. 116) which overwhelms the fox. The death of the animal gives rise to some of Hughes's most disturbing and sensually satisfying imagery:

112

But between us, on the tussocky ground,
Somebody is struggling with something.
An elegant gentleman, beautifully dressed,
Is struggling there, tangled with something,
And biting at something
With his flashing mouth. It is himself
He is tangled with. I come close
As if I might be of help. . . .

                              He has no time for me.
Blood beneath him is spoiling
The magnificent sooted russet
Of his overcoat, and the flawless laundering
Of his shirt. He is desperate
To get himself up on his feet,
And if he could catch the broken pain
In his teeth, and pull it out of his shoulder,
He still has some hope, because
The long brown grass is the same . . . (*WT*, p. 117)

The magic of hooking up the powerful circuit of Nature also includes killing. But who is this gentlemen that dies, who 'has no time for me'? The hunter or the fox? The Australian friend, the noble fox or both of them in the Schoolteacher's mind? Here the dialectic of perspectives works well (and I think older children will probably feel as 'thrown' momentarily as will adults). But what is the relationship between the dialectic of the fox-hunt story and the other dialogue, between the Schoolteacher and the son of God, which the reader will still have in the back of his mind? Indeed this dialogue itself takes place within another dialogue, between all of us and God. How do they all mesh together?

If any one feeling crystallizes in this labyrinth of self-questioning, it is less the psychology of the evil eye than the heavy arguing of an inquisitor who everywhere senses something a bit corrupt. In another of the Schoolteacher's tales, we meet a goat that first appeared in *The Hawk in the Rain*, in the poem 'Meeting' (*HR*, p. 39). There its eye was seen 'shrinking the whole / Sun-swung zodiac of light to a trinket shape'. In *What is the Truth?*:

The Billy Goat passed
Like a nuclear blast.

Out of the dusty fall of Babylon the Great
Walked the Goat, still searching for something to eat.

Out of the tombs of Egypt stepped forth
The Goat, chewing a scrap of mummy cloth.

Into the cave, from which Christ's body had flown,
The Goat peered, evil-eyed, with his horns on.

Whenever a goat stops eating
And aims at you with his nose
Remember the deserts waiting
Between his dirty toes. (*WT*, pp. 79–81)

If we follow the various narrative presences closely we might feel that the Schoolteacher here is disabusing the son of God of any foolish humanized or metaphysical notions he may have. His goat, in other words, is indirectly telling the son of God not to try another Jesus – another transfiguration of the body into a God the Spirit. Moreover, as we pick up and respond to the voices of the goat and his foil, the ideal religions which come and go, we learn the dangers of living in a reality that is not part of the ever-eating, indestructible goat. His grave (not Christianity's) will be the holy ground that is left when all of our churches fall to rubble.

This is, again and again, the message to our non-God selves, and it is a familiar one. The only difference in *What is the Truth?* is that we really do not have a handle to grasp, a clear, recurring set of personas through which we can enter the book as a whole. Perhaps Ted Hughes wanted to treat the general dramatic setting of witnessing before God and his son as a 'mechanical sorter' for the poems (as he said he did for *Crow*). It is true that there is little overall development, but neither is there an overall relationship between the souls of the village folk, their stories, the education of the son of God and God himself.

If anything we lose sight of the radiant pastoral images and the occasional psychodramas. The recurring tenor is one of a rather nasty (rhetorically nasty in any event) God, who is mainly an intimidating person, frowning or carping. Apropos the Farmer's daughter's story, God quips, '"It isn't the Truth either . . . neither the whole Truth nor half the Truth. Even so, it's closer to the Truth than her father or brother"' (*WT*, p. 21). We see Him frowning at the Farmer (*WT*, p. 30) and at the Shepherd (*WT*, p. 42). One could say that Hughes gives us here the God of the world before Christianity kicked the Nature out of Job (Interview I, p. 8). In the person of God, Nature is certainly powerful and demanding, but, as eloquence, it comes across as more heavy-handed and assertive than insidious and engaging. When God sums up His colossal Truth, the feeling for us and His son must be rather like the message given by a drop of water to the man seeking experience (*HR*, pp. 37–8), the 'world-shouldering monstrous "I"'. This is the Truth we take away from *What is the Truth?*: '"I AM ALL THESE THINGS"', God says, in big, black print, *all* the world – fox, rat, lobworm, weasel and cat.

The only consolation we have, at the end of the village testimony, is that *now* the son of God seems to have decided to leave God and dwell amongst us. Whether this is an earned or unearned result is not clear, though the message, God *is* and life is about *being*, does bring most of the characters' preoccupations into an objective focus, for from now on the son of God will stay on earth, ever fascinated, ever listening to our confessions (to him, to ourselves).

As a book bound by an integument of feeling, ideas and subjective and objective focus, *River* is perhaps Hughes's finest collection to date. The legacy or fundamental truth of the Fall or of the parietal lobes is not dismissed, and Hughes is far from changing his basic intuitions about *Homo sapiens*. But now the role of the advocate does change significantly, away from exorcism towards submission, from Dr Jekyll's brain riddles to a compliant sympathy with the animal Hyde – with the sympathetic nervous system of body and Nature. In such submission and in the sympathetic husbandry that seems to go with it, Hughes just turns his back on the old problem of the brain god. This is important to bear in mind if one is to see both the changes in parts of *Moortown* and in parts of *What is the Truth?* and in all of *River* as well as the continuity. The poet simply surrenders to sensations: as the inner drama recedes, the importance of poetry as description grows, but a description where ideal interference is so reduced as to let

Nature become radiant before it becomes symbolic. The threat of the brain god Logos of old is simply overwhelmed by the evidence of the surface of things, including the surface of the arch organ of duplicity, the eye: more than elsewhere, in *River* one feels that Hughes accepts, without a grudge, the possibility that the eye can be a purely or at least a dominantly *sensual* organ rather than an organ of fore- and hind-sight, of aprons and of peekaboo.

In this way the focus of mythic activity shifts from exorcism and questing to dedication and chanting celebration. *River* winds in and out of modes sometimes thought of as contrasting: naturalism, romance, ecstasy – the first being the empire of sensual detail, the second the total suspension of this detail. In point of fact the contrast is not felt at all. Hughes is profoundly naturalistic and sensual. The romance and ecstasy in *River* derive simply from a clarity of detail, from a sacred immanence which experience (in looking and describing) makes palpable. From an idealist point of view, *River* could be said to mark a total collapse of the imagination – very much as, in the diary poems of 'Moortown', a flatness and an absence of dramatic tension reflect a refusal or an unwillingness to symbolize and to interiorize sensations. But since imagination is, as ever for Hughes, bound to the demon god-of-the-parietal-lobes (this is part of the new book's continuity with past work), the 'collapse' is in fact a submission to numbness and a hooking up with the sympathetic nervous system of the world.

Both subjectively and objectively, *River* is more unified than any book Hughes has written to date. Every poem, that is, deals with the 'theme', the river. And, though written over a period of about six years (the earliest, 'Whiteness', goes back to 1977), the collection has, throughout, the feel of a design, bringing many aspects of the river and its banks into one winding source of life during the course of a solstitial year – from the day before Christmas (the first poem) to the day of birth (the last poem). Celebration or praise gathers in all other feelings as Hughes sings, in the best poems, in a world without shadows and without depth – all light, all surface. *River* is a naturalist Psalter. Where the stark, black-and-white photographs of *Remains of Elmet* suggested a quest through memory for symbols and values as mysterious and as pregnant as the characters and spaces of some ancient text, the many lush colour photographs by Peter Keen complement a new endeavour – to tell about a real world that exists, fully adequate, right before the eyes. Following the 'focus' of the poetry, the photographs pass themselves from documentation to ecstasy, from close-ups of a leaping salmon, a hawk-moth or a hawthorn berry to an orgy of glimmers, coruscations and movement. Though the poet and the photographer hardly work together, page to page, as Hughes and Fay Godwin did in *Remains of Elmet*, the mood that settles over *River*, in pictures and words, is unified.

Though Hughes writes of an eel, a cormorant, a kingfisher and the flora and fauna of a number of specific rivers in Britain, Ireland and the Arctic, one creature matters more than any other – the salmon. It is easy to understand why: the salmon virtually creates the poem for the poet; it is, itself, in Ezra Pound's sense, very nearly the adequate symbol, living out before the eyes the unity of death, birth and marriage, in one place, in one moment. The motto of the salmon, swimming against the stream, could well be the motto of the Psalter itself: '*Only birth matters*', a line in italics from the last poem, 'Salmon Eggs' (*R*, p. 124). In the most successful poems of *River*, Hughes uses a nylon thread of narrative, diary-like and unobtrusive, to glide from anecdote to description to identification with what is going on in the natural world – usually something to do with self-perpetuation: 'only birth matters'. Without the narrative to conduct us into such highly charged emotional zones, some of the praise in *River* sounds unearned and assertive.

The first poem uses this narrative line to tell about a visit to a salmon hatchery. The hen's eggs, then the cock's milt are squeezed out into a plastic bucket. The mixture sets, is washed and is sent back into the crashing waters of a weir: 'In natural times', says Hughes, 'those six, with luck, / In five years, with great luck, might make nine' (*R*, p. 12). Through husbandry, the eggs and the milt of a few fish make thousands. Naturalistic sexuality and conniving midwifery – here and in a few other poems – slip into a higher gear of cheery hermaphroditism, where doubles and sexes merge into the essential unity which all but the purest, sensual vision obscures – where molecules mix and 'inner' atoms commune with 'outer' ones, and the poet and reader (himself hooked to the poet's nylon line) converge:

117

Sanctus Sanctus
Swathes the blessed issue.

Perpetual mass
Of the waters
Wells from the cleft.

It is the swollen vent
Of the nameless
Teeming inside atoms – and inside the haze
And inside the sun and inside the earth.
It is the font, brimming with touch and whisper
Swaddling the egg. (*R*, pp. 122–4)

This is a world that literally communes with man, the cellular body, through a process akin to osmosis. A pre-Christmas poem, a ritual for bringing on the day of regeneration and so the whole new cycle of life, the first poem of *River* ends at a point the very last one picks up:

A world
Wrought in wet, heavy gold. Treasure-solid.
That morning
Dazzle-stamped every cell in my body
With its melting edge, its lime-bitter brightness. (*R*, p. 12)

The simple, sensual sight of the salmon's death, as the selvaged edge of life, evokes an identification and a mental numbness that is, psychologically, effortless.

In one of Hughes's most fascinating and complex poems in *River*, 'Gulkana', the old Hughes, the poet of the evil eye of the hawk and of Scout Rock, unexpectedly appears . . . much to the surprise of the 'new' Hughes, who is narrating an experience he recalled whilst returning to England after a fishing trip in Alaska (though we do not realize this until the end of the poem). At the beginning of the poem, the poet tells of a trek he and his companion make over the thawing Arctic lands to where the Copper and the Gulkana rivers meet. First, they pass through a village where a worn-out Indian culture seems to have traded myths and legend for blue jeans. By way of example, he focuses on that part of their mythic lore which subsists now in isolated sounds, pre-Columbian vocables or 'glyphs', like *Gulkana*. What does it mean? The Eskimos haven't a clue, nor at first does the poet. For him, as an angler, *Gulkana* means the headlands of a river where salmon 'too big to eat' run erotically to their death. But *Gulkana* is something else, a mysterious 'glyph' which turns his fishing trip magically into a gesture which fleshes out the enigmatic word. Yet first, as he hobbles up a river, a strange feeling descends: 'I felt hunted . . . fear . . . in my neck . . . in my eyes / Which felt blind somehow to what I stared at / As if it stared at me.'

But there was the eye!
              I peered into that lens
Seeking what I had come for. (What had I come for? . . .

            They were possessed
By that voice in the river,
By the drums and flutes of its volume . . .

Devoured by revelation,
Every molecule seized, and tasted, and drained
Into the amethyst of emptiness –
I came back to myself. (*R*, pp. 82–4)

At just such a moment, the typical interior drama seen so often in Hughes takes off: Body Nature, perceived, begins to stare accusingly at cerebral man, the interloper into prehistory, the spectator of self and world, body and self. In 'Gulkana', however, the ordinary human fool is not pursued but is urged on, up stream, by his own prehistoric double. Moving in this unpronounceable glyph-land, which sounds a 'deranging cry / From the wilderness', the fool begins to *see* his own sensuous origins crystallize as salmon truth: just as the salmon obeys the call of a mesmerizing eros and thanatos, back to the pool of its birth, so our Dante-of-the-fiddling-ways moves magnetically up the Gulkana river towed onwards by the Virgil Nature, to where all things originate and return.

The whole poem can be read, like others in *River*, as pure description: a description of a 'natural' symbol, the salmon. As an anecdote first recalled in a Boeing 747 over 'Greenland's unremoving corpse', the recollection begins with unreal, Americanized 'Cloud-like-a-Boulder' postcard Indians. It develops dramatically with the mention of the creepy stare at the nape and then moves, half mesmerized, half alert, to the glyph and the river that crawls with love-sick fish. The centre of the memory pursues the stare of Nature into the eye of a fish, and this evokes a sympathy which seems to make the 'fool' in the angler disappear. Then, the memory, now a poem, returns to the wakeful self in the aircraft heading yet again to a home of sorts, over a vast, inert body of polar land. Here is the central part of the memory:

> I explained it
> To my quietly arguing, lucid panic
> As my fear of one inside me,
> A bodiless twin, some disinherited being
> And doppelganger other, unliving,
> Everliving, a larva from prehistory
> Whose journey this was,
> Whose gaze I could feel, who now exulted
> Recognizing his home, and who watched me
> Fiddling with my gear – the interloper,
> The fool he had always hated. (*R*, p. 80)

This is quite different from the tensed-up and sublimated fishing in 'Pike', 'For what might move, for what eye might move' (*L*, p. 57). The core of memory is a sort of biological self-lessness, where fish and man, male and female, homeland and prodigal son, move away from opposition into unity. 'Revelation' in this sort of verse is simply diaphanous experience, less a special kind of knowledge than a state of being. In this sense the poem is itself a vision seen through the eye of Nature, the extraordinary sensuous and active eye that unifies sensation and movement and which seeps right into the fiddling angler's optical nerve. For the passenger in the aircraft, the glyph *Gulkana* has become a hieroglyph which brings together past and future into one spontaneity, into a living, mythic vocable, as vibrant in the poem as in the memory of the salmon's eye which, weeks later, is still capable of seducing the 'fool' back into the world of simultaneous birth and death and coextensive self and world.

Writing in a tone that is neither outraged nor psychologically very subversive, Hughes seems in *River* to have acquired a peace of mind that is rarely palpable before. The anecdotal feel seems genuinely to occupy the foreground, and this makes the new poetry all the more subtle and suggestive for being low-key. It will be intriguing to see if *River* represents a new path – for a poet who has now become, at least officially, a public poet – or an alternative path to the 'radical' Hughes of *Crow*, *Cave Birds* and 'Seven Dungeon Songs'.

BIBLIOGRAPHY

PRINCIPAL WORKS BY TED HUGHES

Books

The Hawk in the Rain. London: Faber, 1957. New York: Harper, 1957.

Lupercal. London: Faber, 1960. New York: Harper, 1960.

Meet My Folks! London: Faber, 1961. Indianapolis and New York: Bobbs-Merrill, 1973.

How the Whale Became. London: Faber, 1963. New York: Atheneum, 1964.

The Earth-Owl and Other Moon People. London: Faber, 1963. (Published as part of *Moonwhales* in 1976 in the USA.)

Nessie the Mannerless Monster. London: Faber, 1964. US edition: *Nessie the Monster*. Indianapolis and New York: Bobbs-Merrill, 1974.

Wodwo. London: Faber, 1967. New York: Harper, 1967.

Poetry in the Making. London: Faber, 1967. US edition: *Poetry Is*. New York: Doubleday, 1970.

The Iron Man. London: Faber, 1968. US edition: *The Iron Giant*. New York: Harper, 1968.

Seneca's 'Oedipus'. London: Faber, 1969. New York: Doubleday, 1972.

The Coming of the Kings and Other Plays. London: Faber, 1970. US edition: *The Tiger's Bones*. New York: Viking, 1974.

Crow. London: Faber, 1970. New York: Harper, 1971.

Selected Poems 1957–1967. London: Faber, 1972. New York: Harper & Row, 1973.

Season Songs. New York: Viking, 1975. London: Faber, 1976.

Gaudete. London: Faber, 1977. New York: Harper & Row, 1977.

Moon Bells and Other Poems. London: Chatto & Windus, 1978.

Cave Birds. London: Faber, 1978. New York: Viking, 1979. (A limited edition had appeared first in Ilkley: The Scolar Press, 1975.)

Remains of Elmet. London: Faber, 1979. New York: Harper & Row, 1979.

Moortown. London: Faber, 1979. New York: Harper & Row, 1979.
Selected Poems 1957–1981. London: Faber, 1982. New York: Harper & Row, 1982.
River. London: Faber in association with James & James, 1983. New York: Harper & Row, 1984.
What is the Truth? London: Faber, 1984. New York: Harper & Row, 1984.

Articles, interviews, recordings, book reviews and editions

Critically, the most useful pieces are Hughes's two essays on myth, 'Myth and Education' of 1970 and 1976, his two interviews with Egbert Faas of 1971 and 1977, his essays on Shakespeare (1971), Pilinszky (1976) and Popa (1978) and the notes and mythic story that went into the making of *Orghast* (told by A. C. H. Smith in *Orghast at Persepolis*). Also both Sagar, in *The Art of Ted Hughes*, and Gifford and Roberts, in *Ted Hughes, A Critical Study*, quote letters and conversations which are valuable. What follows here are the items that throw the most light on Hughes's development and his art.

Articles

'The Rock' (growing up in the Calder Valley). *The Listener*, 19 September 1963.
'Myth and Education'. *Children's Literature in Education*, 1 (1970).
'Ted Hughes's *Crow*'. *The Listener*, 30 July 1970.
Letter in reply to Christopher Ricks's review of *A Choice of Shakespeare's Verse*. *The Sunday Times*, 23 January 1972.
'Myth and Education'. In G. Fox *et al.* (eds), *Writers, Critics and Children*. London: Heinemann, 1976.

Interviews

'Ted Hughes and *Crow*' (Egbert Faas). *London Magazine*, January 1970.
'Orghast' (Tom Stoppard). *The Times Literary Supplement*, 1 October 1971.
'The Persepolis Follies' (Geoffrey Reeves). *Performance*, 1 (December 1971).
'Playing with Words at Persepolis' (Ossia Trilling). *Theatre Quarterly*, 2,5 (January–March 1972).
'An Interview with British Poet, Ted Hughes, Inventor of Orghast Language' (Jean Richards). *Drama and Theatre*, 10,4 (1972).
Interview, notes and drawing. In A. C. H. Smith, *Orghast at Persepolis*, chs 2 and 3. London: Eyre Methuen, 1972.
'Ted Hughes and *Gaudete*' (Ekbert (*sic*) Faas). In E. Faas, *Ted Hughes: The Unaccommodated Universe*, Appendix II. Santa Barbara, Calif.: Black Sparrow Press, 1980. (The interview dates from 1977.)

Recordings

'Crow' Read by Ted Hughes. Claddagh Records, CCT 9–10, 1973.

The Poetry and Voice of Ted Hughes. Caedmon Records, TC 1535, 1977.

Ted Hughes and R. S. Thomas Read and Discuss Selections of Their Own Poems. Norwich Tapes ('The Critical Forum'), 1978.

Book reviews

Living Free by Joy Adamson and other books. *New Statesman*, 10 November 1961.

The Nerve of Some Animals by Robert Froman and *Man and Dolphin* by J. C. Lilly. *New Statesman*, 23 March 1962.

Primitive Song by C. M. Bowra. *The Listener*, 3 May 1962.

Vagrancy by Philip O'Connor. *New Statesman*, 6 September 1963.

Voss by Patrick White. *The Listener*, 6 February 1964.

Myth and Religion of the North by E. O. Turville-Petre. *The Listener*, 19 March 1964.

Astrology by Louis MacNeice and *Ghost and Divining Rod* by T. C. Lethbridge. *New Statesman*, 2 October 1964.

Shamanism by Mircea Eliade and *The Sufis* by Idries Shah. *The Listener*, 29 October 1964.

The Selected Letters of Dylan Thomas edited by C. Fitzgibbon. *New Statesman*, 25 November 1966.

The Environmental Revolution by Max Nicholson. *Spectator*, 21 March 1970.

A Separate Reality by Carlos Castaneda. *The Observer*, 5 March 1972.

Editions

Introduction to *Selected Poems of Keith Douglas*. London: Faber, 1964.

Introduction to *A Choice of Emily Dickinson's Verse*. London: Faber, 1968.

Introduction to *Selected Poems of Vasko Popa*. Harmondsworth: Penguin, 1969. (Later augmented for *Collected Poems 1943–1976*. Manchester: Carcanet, 1977.)

Introduction and note to *A Choice of Shakespeare's Verse*. London: Faber, 1971. US edition: *With Fairest Flowers While Summer Lasts*. New York: Doubleday, 1971.

Introduction to *Selected Poems of Janos Pilinszky*, trans. with Janos Csokits. Manchester: Carcanet, 1976.

Introduction to *Amen* by Yehuda Amichai. London: Oxford University Press, 1977.

Introduction and notes to *Collected Poems* by Sylvia Plath. London: Faber, 1981.

Foreword and notes to *The Journals of Sylvia Plath*. New York: The Dial Press, 1982.

BIBLIOGRAPHY

Sagar, Keith and Tabor, Stephen. *Ted Hughes: A Bibliography 1946–1980*. London: Mansell, 1983.

SELECTED CRITICISM OF TED HUGHES

Books

Bedient, Calvin. *Eight Contemporary Poets*. London: Oxford University Press, 1974.
Bold, Alan. *Thom Gunn and Ted Hughes*. Edinburgh: Oliver & Boyd, 1976.
Faas, Ekbert (*sic*). *Ted Hughes: The Unaccommodated Universe*. Santa Barbara, Calif.: Black Sparrow Press, 1980. (With interviews and a selection of Hughes's critical writings.)
Gifford, Terry and Roberts, Neil. *Ted Hughes: A Critical Study*. London: Faber, 1981.
Hirschberg, Stuart. *Myth in the Poetry of Ted Hughes*. County Dublin: Wolfhound Press, 1981.
Sagar, Keith. *The Art of Ted Hughes*. 2nd edn, Cambridge: Cambridge University Press, 1978.
—— (ed.). *The Achievement of Ted Hughes*. Manchester: Manchester University Press, 1983. (Sixteen essays on a great variety of aspects of Hughes's works, plus uncollected and unpublished poems.)
Schmidt, Michael. *An Introduction to Fifty Modern British Poets*. London: Pan, 1979.
Uroff, Margaret. *Sylvia Plath and Ted Hughes*. Champaign, Ill.: University of Illinois Press, 1979.
Walder, Dennis. *Ted Hughes and Sylvia Plath*. Milton Keynes: Open University Press, 1976.

Articles

Heaney, Seamus. 'Now and in England' (on Hughes, Geoffrey Hill and Philip Larkin). In *Preoccupations: Selected Prose 1968–1978*. London and Boston, Mass.: Faber, 1980.
Holbrook, David. 'From "Vitalism" to a Dead Crow: Ted Hughes's Failure of Confidence'. In *Lost Bearings in English Poetry*. London: Vision Press, 1977.
Kramer, Lawrence. 'The Wodwo Watches the Water Clock'. *Contemporary Literature*, 18, 3 (1977), pp. 391–42.
Larrissy, Edward. 'Ted Hughes, the Feminine, and *Gaudete*'. *Critical Quarterly*, 25 (Summer 1983), pp. 33–41.
Libby, Anthony. 'God's Lioness and the Priest of Sycorax: Plath and Hughes'. *Contemporary Literature*, 15, 3 (1974), pp. 386–405.

Lodge, David. 'Crow and the Cartoons'. *Critical Quarterly*, 13 (Spring 1971), pp. 37–42 and 68.

May, Derwent. 'Ted Hughes'. In Martin Dodsworth (ed.), *The Survival of Poetry*. London: Faber, 1970.

Morse, Brian, 'Poetry, Children and Ted Hughes'. In Nancy Chambers (ed.), *The Signal Approach to Children's Literature*. Harmondsworth: Kestrel Books, 1980.

Newton, J. M. 'No Longer "Through the Pipes of Greece"?' (about *Gaudete*). *Cambridge Quarterly*, 7, 4 (1977), pp. 335–45.

Rawson, Claude. 'Ted Hughes: A Reappraisal'. *Essays in Criticism*, 15, 1 (1965), pp. 77–94.

Thurley, Geoffrey. 'Beyond Positive Values: Ted Hughes'. In *The Ironic Harvest*. London: Arnold, 1974.